Ernst Denert Award for Software Engineering 2019

Michael Felderer • Wilhelm Hasselbring •
Heiko Koziolek • Florian Matthes • Lutz Prechelt •
Ralf Reussner • Bernhard Rumpe • Ina Schaefer
Editors

Ernst Denert Award for Software Engineering 2019

Practice Meets Foundations

 Springer

Editors
Michael Felderer
Department of Computer Science
University of Innsbruck
Innsbruck, Austria

Wilhelm Hasselbring
Department of Computer Science
Kiel University
Kiel, Germany

Heiko Koziolek
Corporate Research
ABB
Ladenburg, Germany

Florian Matthes
Institute of Computer Science
Technical University Munich
Garching, Germany

Lutz Prechelt
Department of Mathematics
and Computer Science
Freie Universität Berlin
Berlin, Germany

Ralf Reussner
Program Structures and Data Organization
Karlsruhe Institute of Technology
Karlsruhe, Germany

Bernhard Rumpe
Software Engineering
RWTH Aachen University
Aachen, Germany

Ina Schaefer
Software Engineering and Automotive
Informatics
Technische Universität Braunschweig
Braunschweig, Germany

ISBN 978-3-030-58619-5   ISBN 978-3-030-58617-1   (eBook)
https://doi.org/10.1007/978-3-030-58617-1

This book is an open access publication.

This Springer imprint is published by the registered company Springer Nature Switzerland AG.
The registered company address is: Gewerbestrasse 11, 6330 Cham, Switzerland

Contents

Ernst Denert Software Engineering Awards 2019

Michael Felderer, Wilhelm Hasselbring, Heiko Koziolek, Florian Matthes, Lutz Prechelt, Ralf Reussner, Bernhard Rumpe, and Ina Schaefer

Abstract The need to improve software engineering practices is continuously rising and software development practitioners are highly interested in improving their software systems and the methods to build them. And well, software engineering research has numerous success stories. The Ernst Denert Software Engineering Award specifically rewards researchers that value the practical impact of their work and aim to improve current software engineering practices. This chapter summarizes the awards history as well as the current reward process and criteria.

M. Felderer
University of Innsbruck, Innsbruck, Austria
e-mail: michael.felderer@uibk.ac.at

W. Hasselbring
Department of Computer Science, Kiel University, Kiel, Germany
e-mail: wha@informatik.uni-kiel.de

H. Koziolek
ABB, Ladenburg, Germany
e-mail: heiko.koziolek@de.abb.com

F. Matthes
Institute of Computer Science, Technical University Munich, Garching, Germany
e-mail: matthes@in.tum.de

L. Prechelt
Department of Mathematics and Computer Science, Freie Universität Berlin, Berlin, Germany
e-mail: prechelt@inf.fu-berlin.de

R. Reussner
Karlsruhe Institute of Technology, Karlsruhe, Germany
e-mail: reussner@kit.edu

B. Rumpe (✉)
RWTH Aachen University, Aachen, Germany
e-mail: rumpe@se-rwth.de

I. Schaefer
Technische Universität Braunschweig, Braunschweig, Germany
e-mail: i.schaefer@tu-bs.de

© The Author(s) 2020
M. Felderer et al. (eds.), *Ernst Denert Award for Software Engineering 2019*,
https://doi.org/10.1007/978-3-030-58617-1_1

1   Relevance of Software Engineering

The need to improve software engineering practices is continuously rising. While commercial software systems in the 1980s and 1990s typically comprised a few hundred thousand lines of code, Windows 10 today has more than 50 million lines of code. Google's code base size is estimated at more than 2 billion lines of code, where thousands of software developers are contributing. There are more than 20 million professional software developers in the world, and in the USA they already make up 2.5% of the entire workforce. Recent technology advances in connectivity and artificial intelligence create a plethora of ever-growing software systems that are impossible to manage without sound software engineering practices.

Software engineering research had numerous success stories in the past. Design patterns experienced by practitioners were codified by academics and became an important communication tool for developers across the world. The Representational State Transfer (REST) architecture style captures key principles for designing web services and was a fundamental contribution to the world wide web. The ACM Impact Project traced back the design of many commercial middleware products to Ph.D. theses on distributed computing from the 1970s. Similar investigations were done for programming languages, configuration management, code walkthroughs, and exception handling. While it is still relatively rare that the output of a software engineering Ph.D. thesis is directly commercialized, the concepts and ideas sometimes influence commercial products indirectly, and the impact on software engineering practices is visible only much later.

Software development practitioners are highly interested in improving their software systems and the methods to build them. Microsoft Research interviewed 3000 Microsoft developers on how they viewed the practical relevance of academic works in the field. In general, the developers consider the best works in the field positive and are looking for ways to integrate them into their daily work. However, some research ideas are also characterized as "unwise," for example tools that are not needed, empirical studies that produce no actionable outcome, methods that are tuned for very specific contexts, approaches that incur such high costs that they outweigh the benefits.

Therefore, the Ernst Denert Software Engineering Award specifically rewards researchers that value the practical impact of their work and aim to improve current software engineering practices. Creating tighter feedback loops between professional practitioners and academic researchers is essential to make research ideas ready for industry adoption. Researchers who demonstrate their proposed methods and tools on non-trivial systems under real-world conditions shall be supported, so that the gap between research and practice can be decreased.

2 History of the Ernst Denert Software Engineering Award

"Passion Software-Engineering." This was the headline of a 2015 newspaper article about Ernst Denert. And they were absolutely right. Ernst Denert (Fig. 1) is really passionate about developing software with excellent quality in a predictable and systematic style. His seminal book on Software-Engineering in 2001,[1] the famous "Black Book on Software-Engineering" is depicted in Fig. 2. This book was the basis for software development projects at the company *sd&m* as well as teaching courses in practical application of software development techniques to industrial projects.

Fig. 1 Ernst Denert

Ernst Denert furthermore is very much interested in encouraging young people to study computer science or at least to learn how programming and digitalization works, but also computer science students to concentrate on software engineering principles and software development. Starting with a degree in communications engineering he early moved to computer science in his Ph.D. thesis at TU Berlin, where software engineering was already an issue.

Then he went to industry and relatively soon started together with colleagues the already mentioned software development company "sd&m" (Software Design and Management) in 1982. He headed the company until 2001, when he left for a new endeavor, namely CEO of the IVU Traffic Technologies AG. He thus moved from individual software development projects to a software product house.

Ernst Denert was always passionate on Software Engineering. That was why he also was active in teaching at the Munich University of Technology in 1991, where he also received an Honorary Professorship position and also founded the Ernst

---

[1] Ernst Denert: Software-Engineering, Springer Berlin, 1991.

Fig. 2 Software Engineering
by Ernst Denert[2]

Denert Software Engineering price back in 1989. The price was at first funded by the Ernst Denert Stiftung and now is funded by the Gerlind & Ernst Denert Stiftung.

The software engineering community greatfully thanks the Gerlind & Ernst Denert Stiftung for their continuous support of the community.

As said: It was always an important topic for Professor Denert to push forward the field of Software Engineering. This was therefore logical to run a special conference on Software Engineering to bring together the most influential Software Engineering Pioneers and also publish a proceedings of that happening (Fig. 3).[4]

Currently, Ernst Denert is also funding and working on a project called "Vitruv,"[5] where we can expect a book on software architecture to emerge. We are looking forward to see many more interesting things to come.

---

[2]From https://www.springer.com/de/book/9783642843440.

[3]From https://www.springer.com/de/book/9783540430810.

[4]Software Pioneers. Contributions to Software Engineering. Published by Manfred Broy and Ernst Denert, Springer, 2002.

[5]https://software-architecture.org/.

Fig. 3 Software Pioneers[3]

3 Award Submission Process

For the 2019 and forthcoming awards, the criteria have changed slightly, the organization was taken over by the GI, and the form of presentation of the nominated works has been extended by this book. The call for submissions to the 2019 awards was roughly as follows.

The Ernst Denert Software Engineering Award for outstanding contributions to the Software Engineering discipline is awarded by the

- Fachbereich Softwaretechnik of the German Society for Informatics (GI), the
- Suisse Society for Informatics (SI), and the
- Austrian Computing Society (OCG).

The award is given annually and endowed with 5,000 Euros. We gratefully thank the *Gerlind & Ernst Denert-Stiftung* for the kind donation of the price and takeover of the financial costs for the colloquium.

The prize is awarded for excellent work within the discipline of Software Engineering, which includes methods, tools, and procedures for better and efficient development of high quality software that was created in the area of SI, OCG, or GI.

An essential requirement is applicability and usability in industrial practice. The practical applicability must be demonstrated. Open source software or results published as open data are welcome, but commercial products are excluded.

Proposals can be sent by (1) scientific universities in Germany, Austria, and Switzerland that have the right to confer doctorates in computer science. Universities may propose dissertations and habilitations. All work with a final examination in the period from September 1 to August 31 is permitted. (2) Proposals can also be sent by all software engineers—these are typically members of one of the Software Engineering divisions within the GI, SI, or OCG. They may propose academic or non-academic work that they consider worthwhile. This particularly includes work in the area of open source or open data with relevance to the Software Engineering field.

Deadline for a proposal in 2019 was December 15.

For dissertations and postdoctoral theses the following documents have been submitted: dissertation (resp. habilitation), justification of the proposal by the submitting software engineer/university, the reports of the reviewing experts, whereby at least one review was prepared by an independent expert, a curriculum vitae of the Doctoral candidate including a list of publications, and a link to the corresponding doctoral regulations of the university.

For open source and open data projects the submission had to include a project description, justification of the proposal by the submitting software engineer, a laudatio of at least one independent expert, a curriculum vitae of the project members involved, a list of publications referring to the project, links on the sources of the published results (e.g., an open data directory), and installation and usage instructions.

4 Selection Criteria

The jury discussed extensively the criteria to be applied to the submissions and agreed on the following list of considerations:

1. Above all is the potential to contribute to a better software engineering practice. Practical applicability of the results is therefore a conditio sine qua non.
2. This applicability needs to be demonstrated (or, if long timescales are involved, at least demonstrated to be likely).
3. Contributions may aim to be useful directly, e.g., via a tool, or indirectly via theoretical or empirical insights.
4. They may target the software product or the software development process.
5. They may pertain to "hot" topics or to eternal problems of software development.
6. They may promise large improvements ("tenfold") in narrow domains of applicability or incremental improvements in broad domains. Domains of applicability can be narrow or broad with respect to technology assumptions, development process assumptions, assumptions regarding the target software application domain, or the set of software development tasks being addressed.
7. These criteria will lead to the need of comparing apples to oranges. When comparing dissimilar contributions in a neck-and-neck race, the jury will favor more credible packages over more impressive ones.
8. The best submissions are those that will be viewed as important steps forward even 15 years from now.

9. This is not a Ph.D. dissertation price. Submissions can come from individuals or groups, can take any form, may cover longer or shorter time spans, and do not even need to be framed as research.

5 Selection Process

From the submitted proposal the jury, which is identical to the editors of this book, selected an appropriate subset of candidates.

The selected *"Ernst Denert Software Engineering Award Nominees,"* were asked to present their results and further empirical findings in the form of a colloquium that took place in January 15th to 17th, 2020 in the Leibniz Center for Computer Science at Schloss Dagstuhl (Fig. 4).

Fig. 4 The nominees and the committee in Dagstuhl[6]

All nominated candidates and especially the winning person (or group) are invited to summarize their work in this book.

Further information can be found on the webpage of the Software Engineering community of the GI.[7]

6 The Award Nominees and the Winner

Based on the nominations that have been received, the following list of nominees was selected and invited to a two day Dagstuhl seminar. Each of the candidates had the possibility to present and defend her or his thesis in front of the committee (in alphabetical order):

---

[6]From https://www.dagstuhl.de/20033.

[7]https://fb-swt.gi.de/ernst-denert-se-preis.

- Sebastian Baltes, Universität Trier
  was nominated by his university with his doctoral thesis on *Software Developers' Work Habits and Expertise*. His doctor father was Stephan Diehl, his second examiner Stefan Wagner.
- Timo Greifenberg, RWTH Aachen
  was nominated by his university with his doctoral thesis on *Artefaktbasierte Analyse modellgetriebener Softwareentwicklungsprojekte*. His doctor father was Bernhard Rumpe, his second examiner Steffen Becker.
- Marco Konersmann, Universität Duisburg-Essen
  was nominated by his university with his doctoral thesis on *Explicitly Integrated Architecture*. His doctor father was Michael Goedicke, his second examiner Ralf Reussner.
- Marija Selakovic, Technischen Universität Darmstadt
  was nominated by her university with her doctoral thesis on *Actionable Program Analyses for Improving Software Performance*. Her doctor father was Michael Pradel, her second examiner Frank Tip.
- Johannes Späth, Paderborn University
  was nominated by his university with his doctoral thesis on *Synchronized Pushdown Systems for Pointer and Data-Flow Analysis*. His doctor father was Eric Bodden, his second examiner Karim Ali.

We congratulate *Johannes Späth*, his doctoral supervisor *Eric Bodden*, and Paderborn University for winning the Ernst Denert Software Engineering Award 2019.

Johannes had the possibility to present the most important results of his thesis called *Synchronized Pushdown Systems for Pointer and Data-Flow Analysis* during his talk at the software engineering conference SE 2020 from February 24 to 28, 2020, Innsbruck, Austria and of course also in Chapter 3 of this book.

Fig. 5 Award ceremony in Innsbruck: Professor Denert and Dr. Späth

Figure 5 shows the laudator Professor Denert handing over the award certificate to the award winner Johannes Späth after the presentation.

7 Contents of the Book

All the nominees were given the chance to present in the following chapters

- the key findings of the work,
- their relevance and applicability to practice and industrial software engineering projects, and
- additional information and findings that have only been discovered afterwards, e.g., when applying the results in industry.

Software Engineering projects are teamwork. In practice outstanding accident research is also teamwork. This somewhat conflicts with the requirement that a doctoral thesis is a monograph. To reflect the teamwork idea, quite like Professor Denert is discussing in Chap. 2, we decided that the following papers, describing this research can (or should even) be written with co-authors that somehow contributed to the findings during the thesis development or continue to work with the results.

7.1 Thanks

We gratefully thank Professor Ernst Denert for all his help in the process and the *Gerlind & Ernst Denert Stiftung* for the kind donation of the price and takeover of the financial costs for the colloquium. We also thank all the people helping in the organization, including Katrin Hölldobler for managing the submission and the selection process, the colloquium, and the book organization. We thank the organization team of Castle Dagstuhl, whose customary overwhelming hospitality allowed us to run the colloquium. Furthermore, we thank the organization team of the software engineering conference SE 2020 to host the award ceremony in Innsbruck. Finally, we thank the GI, the OCG, and the SI computer science societies and especially their Software Engineering divisions for their support in making this price a success.

Software Engineering

Ernst Denert

Abstract "A Passion for Software-Engineering." This was the headline of a 2015 newspaper article about Ernst Denert. And they were absolutely right. Ernst Denert is really passionate about developing software with excellent quality in a predictable and systematic style. Furthermore, he is very much interested in encouraging young people to study computer science or at least to learn how programming and digitalization works, as well as computer science students to focus on software engineering principles and software development. This chapter is a personal view of Ernst Denert on the software engineering discipline.

A personal view on the Software Engineering discipline.

1 1968

"What we need, is software engineering," said F.L. Bauer in 1968, and he organized the conference in Garmisch that founded our profession. The following is a translation of an excerpt from his report (available only in German) on this conference in the Informatik-Spektrum[1] 25 years later:

> One day, annoyed by the fact that in the end, nothing more than yet another pure academic project could emerge, I commented: "The whole trouble comes from the fact that there is so much tinkering with software. It is not made in a clean fabrication process, which it should be." Noticing that this shocked some of my colleagues, I added: "What we need, is software engineering." That made an impact.

---

[1] Quoted from F.L. Bauer: Software Engineering—wie es begann, (Software Engineering—How it Began) Informatik-Spektrum, Oct. 1993, page 259.

E. Denert (✉)
Grünwald, Germany

© The Author(s) 2020
M. Felderer et al. (eds.), *Ernst Denert Award for Software Engineering 2019*,
https://doi.org/10.1007/978-3-030-58617-1_2

11

The official conference report[2] recorded the following:

The phrase 'software engineering' was deliberately chosen as being provocative, in imply-
ing the need for software manufacture to be based on the types of theoretical foundations
and practical disciplines, that are traditional in the established branches of engineering.

The aim was that software development should become an engineering discipline
with a systematic method of working, roughly according to the schema

plan—design—produce—check—install—maintain.

Just like a house needs a construction plan and a machine needs a design drawing,
so a software system needs an architecture.

2 Software Architecture

Software architecture is the supreme discipline of software engineering. It covers
the design of software systems as a whole, with their technical functionality and
the interfaces to the outside world, as well as the internal structure at every level of
detail. At a high level, software architecture is concerned with the construction of
a system made up of modules, the interaction between these modules in executable
processes, and the distribution of the system over hardware components. At a
detailed level, software architecture is concerned with the design of individual
modules: on the one hand, with their external view, that is, their interface to other
modules, and on the other hand, with their internal structure, that is, which functions
operate on which data.

In IT, the word "architecture" has become established as a "superior" designation
for various types of structures, and this is also true in the case of software. Software
architecture is a buzzword that is much overused. It has many interpretations, with
the understanding sometimes being that architecture in itself is something good.
That is not true—some architecture is bad. Sometimes we hear, "Our software has
no architecture." That is also not correct; every system has an architecture. What is
generally meant is that the structure of the system is poor or inconsistent, it exists
undocumented only in the minds of some programmers or is completely unknown.
Nevertheless, it does exist.

Such structures are frequently represented in graphic form with boxes and lines
between the boxes, mostly without defining precisely what they mean. The boxes
represent components, modules, functions, files, and processes; the lines and arrows
represent various types of relationship, references, data flows, calls, and much more.
There is often no consensus over them, not even within a project, a department, and

---

[2]SOFTWARE ENGINEERING, Report on a conference sponsored by the NATO SCIENCE
COMMITTEE, Garmisch, Germany, Oct. 7–11, 1968, chapter 1, page 13.

certainly not within whole commercial businesses, and just as little in scientific institutions.

My definition of *software architecture* is that it is the static and dynamic structures that shape a software system, considered from three perspectives, referred to as *views*: the application, design, and program views. We think about the system differently in each view. And thinking needs language. All people think in their native language, musicians think in notes, architects think in drawings, medical professionals think in Latin terms, mathematicians think in formulas. And programmers think in programming languages. However, that is not enough to design software architecture; each view has its own terminology, concepts, and forms of presentation:

2.1 Application View

For this view, we have to understand the language of the users and think in concepts and the terminology of the application, regardless of the type of the application (business, technical, scientific, media, etc.). In *business* systems, this view is concerned with data, technical functionality, and business processes, as well as interaction with users (dialogs) and neighboring systems; in *technical* systems, the view is concerned with the physical machinery and control processes. Technical content is described with natural language and more or less formal representations.

2.2 Design View

This view is concerned with the modular design of a software system—that is, its construction from modules with their static and dynamic relationships. Graphical representations are very popular, both informal ones as well as those with formal syntax and semantics, such as UML. Natural language is also used here. On the one hand, the technical concepts of the application view shape the design; they should be clearly recognizable in the design. On the other hand, the design defines the system platform that the software runs on.

2.3 Program View

Here, formal languages dominate programming languages, interfaces of frameworks and libraries (APIs), and communication protocols. The development environment and tools, as well as programming rules, shape the method of working. The high-level program structures are predetermined by the design; in particular, the directory structure of the source code is predetermined by the modularization.

At first glance, the architecture views look like *development phases*. They can be seen as such, but I consider the architecture of a software system primarily in terms of the result—that is, what it is or what it should be—rather than in terms of how it is created. Just imagine, a ready-to-use software system has to be approved before it is used, just like trains, new models of automobiles, or medical devices. The test required for this purpose examines the system's *actual* architecture, based on its documentation and above all how it is manifested in code; it does not examine how the system has been created. In this results-based examination, development processes and procedure models are not important—regardless of whether they are agile or based on phases.

We are repeatedly faced with the differentiation between "rough" and "detailed," such as the differentiation between a rough specification and a detailed specification. This is useful if the rough form is a precise abstraction of the detailed form, but not if rough means only "thereabouts." A rough presentation is also good if it gives a good overview of complex content with a lot of details. However, the application view must in no way be understood as rough, with the design view being a refinement of the application view. Precise details are important in all views.

3 Software Development

Engineering-based software development is of course based on an architecture plan, but in practice there is still a lot of "tinkering" (F.L. Bauer) even today, although this is now referred to as being "agile."

Over the decades, many concepts for processes in software projects have been published and practiced. Various designations based on graphical representations have been defined for the structured process in phases: waterfall model, spiral model, and V model. These metaphors are not significantly enlightening in terms of facts, but they are the object of ideological discussions.

In large organizations, and state organizations in particular, there is a tendency to implement phase and maturity models in a formal, bureaucratic way. The best-known examples are the Capability Maturity Model (CMMI) of the Software Engineering Institute (SEI) in the USA and the German V model. On the other hand, and as a countermovement, a good 20 years ago agile methods came into being, starting with Extreme Programming (XP) and today, primarily Scrum.

Making a plan is an alien concept to proponents of agile; writing down requirements and an architecture design is deemed to be a waste of time and effort. Instead, in a series of steps, mostly referred to as sprints, something is instantly programmed that could be useful to the user. If this gives rise to bungled program structures, refactoring is conducted. That is strange: we do not think about the software structure at the beginning, but when it is ruined after multiple programming sprints, we start to repair it. That is not a structured way of working. There is no engineering-based methodology in the agile methods; consequently, the Scrum guide makes no mention of software engineering.

In his book "Agile!," Bertrand Meyer offers a profound, factual presentation, analysis, and assessment of the agile methods. I have only one thing to add to this, the best thing about the agile methods is their name: agile—a terrific marketing gag. Who dares to say, we are not agile, we work in a structured way?

In a nutshell: regardless of how a team works—with an engineering method, using agile methods, or in some other way—*thought must be given to the software architecture*. It can be designed before programming and written down, or ingeniously hacked into the code—*but the software architecture must have been thought about*. In the end, something is definitely written down—in the code. Hopefully, it works. *In code veritas*.

4   Teamwork

Software systems are complex and large; they can consist of hundreds of thousands or even millions of lines of code. They cannot be developed by one person alone; teamwork is required. This requires structure—in the software, an architecture and in the team, a division of tasks. Not everyone can do everything at any time.

Recently, teamwork has been idealized: mixed groups, with no manager, in flat hierarchies, acting under their own responsibility and self-organizing, they achieve everything easily in daily standup meetings, from sprint to sprint. Deep and thorough contemplation by individuals—for example, about aspects of architecture such as the modularity of a software—is not required. The German Wikipedia article about Scrum states the following: "The development team is responsible ... for delivery ... is self-organizing."

Responsibility cannot be ascribed to a team; it can only be ascribed to individual persons. And a professional project team does not come together like a group of friends organizing a party; it is initially put together by someone with personnel responsibility. If there are no further specifications, an informal organization does arise along with leadership, but there are no clear, binding responsibilities. A friend of mine caricatures it with the following saying: "Team = **T**oll, **e**in **a**nderer **m**acht's" (great, somebody else will do it).

In contrast, one of the fundamental experiences of my (professional) life is that people want to and must be led. Of course, the military type of leadership with command and obedience does not come into question for software developers; it is more like that of a football trainer of a professional team or the conductor of a symphony orchestra. A project lead must be convincing and must have the professional skill to instruct employees in both a communicative and a motivational way and to ensure that they (can) achieve good results. On the occasion of the

25th anniversary of the Software Engineering Conference in Garmisch, I wrote
something in an Informatik-Spektrum article that still holds true today[3]:

> Good team spirit is more important for the success of a software project than all
> technology. Therefore, management must constantly strive to ensure conditions for a
> good atmosphere—a manager must create a good quality of working life. Of course, the
> atmosphere can only arise in the team itself, with everyone contributing to it; the better the
> communication and understanding, the better the atmosphere.

5 A Final Wish

Looking back over a quarter of a century of the Software Engineering Prize showed
me that a large part of the work is concerned with analytical processes, such as
analyzing code and models, but design methods rarely appear. This is regrettable,
because software engineering is the doctrine of shaping, designing, building, and
developing software systems. Why is there no software engineering school at some
universities that states, by way of a standard: This is how you should do it? I would
be happy for there to be two or three that compete with one another, possibly with
each having a different orientation with regard to the types of systems, be they
technical, operational, or media systems.

Is it down to the lack of practical relevance or the short-winded academic
life, in which primarily six-page articles are published with the aim of improving
the citation index? Textbooks are now rarely written. I would like a constructive
software engineering doctrine, as a book, available on paper and of course digitally,
supplemented by a website with code examples and further materials.

Most Computer Science graduates who go into business practice work on
developing software—for new systems as well as existing ones. Such a doctrine
should serve to accompany them on their journey, explaining specifically how to
develop. We may then hear in companies, "We follow the X school"—that would
be something.

And it could help software engineering, our practical and very relevant discipline,
gain standing in the public view again, from which, just like Computer Science, it
has disappeared, overrun by the ubiquitous buzzwords.

---

[3]E. Denert: Software-Engineering in Wissenschaft und Wirtschaft: Wie breit ist die Kluft?
(Software Engineering in Science and Business: How Wide Is the Gap?) Informatik-Spektrum,
Oct. 1993, page 299.

Applications of Synchronized Pushdown Systems

Johannes Späth

Abstract A precise static data-flow analysis transforms the program into a context-sensitive and field-sensitive approximation of the program. It is challenging to design an analysis of this precision efficiently due to the fact that the analysis is undecidable per se. Synchronized pushdown systems (SPDS) present a highly precise approximation of context-sensitive and field-sensitive data-flow analysis. This chapter presents some data-flow analyses that SPDS can be used for. Further on, this chapter summarizes two other contributions of the thesis "Synchronized Pushdown System for Pointer and Data-Flow Analysis" called BOOMERANG and IDE^{al}. BOOMERANG is a demand-driven pointer analysis that builds on top of SPDS and minimizes the highly computational effort of a whole-program pointer analysis by restricting the computation to the minimal program slice necessary for an individual query. IDE^{al} is a generic and efficient framework for data-flow analyses, e.g., typestate analysis. IDE^{al} resolves pointer relations automatically and efficiently by the help of BOOMERANG. This reduces the burden of implementing pointer relations into an analysis. Further on, IDE^{al} performs strong updates, which makes the analysis sound and precise.

1 Introduction

Our economy as well as our society more and more depends on software solutions. In the era of digitalization almost every company hires software developers to build new or integrate existing software solutions to improve workflows and thus the company's productivity, and to monitor processes or experiment with new business models. The increase in demand also increases the amount of software code written.

Additionally, companies move their solutions to cloud resources and let them exchange sensitive data between internal or external services and company machines and desktop computers. The demand in cloud services simplifies cyber-

J. Späth (✉)
Paderborn University, Paderborn, Germany

© The Author(s) 2020
M. Felderer et al. (eds.), *Ernst Denert Award for Software Engineering 2019*,
https://doi.org/10.1007/978-3-030-58617-1_3

19

attacks. The services are reachable from within a network. Therefore no service can trust *any* user input, and security must be also taken care of at implementation level.

Spotting security bugs on the software implementation level, however, is a cumbersome task and extremely challenging, even for experts. It is frequently a chain of events within the software that attackers abuse to access the system. Take for example a SQL injection attack; a SQL injection allows an attacker to read, manipulate, or even delete contents of a database. First, this attack requires a hacker to be able to manipulate external input data and second, the execution of a SQL command that relies on the manipulated data. Therefore, it is the combination of at least two lines of code that contribute to software being vulnerable to a SQL injection attack. Modern software projects commonly consist of hundreds of thousands to millions of lines of code [7, 19, 36], and finding the right sequence of events manually is near to impossible, particularly because most parts of modern software are third-party libraries that are developed externally.

This advocates for automated solutions to detect security bugs in code. Static data-flow analysis is one automated technique. Apart from many applications in compilers and bug detection [16, 31, 43], a static data-flow analysis has the capability to detect SQL injections directly within the code base [27, 29]. In general, static data-flow analysis reasons about the flow of program variables within the software without executing it, which means static analysis can be applied and used before the software is even tested. Static analysis can, at least in theory, trace all data-flows along all potential execution paths within software and hereby provides provable guarantees that the analysis does not miss a single pattern it is looking for. This is a helpful property from a security perspective, where missing a single security bug suffices for an attacker to take over the whole system.

However, the size of modern software applications not only challenge manual inspection but even limit automated static data-flow analyses. Static analyses are said to be imprecise and slow. They generate a large amount of false warnings and take hours or days to complete. In all cases, neither developers nor security experts are willing to use data-flow techniques on a daily basis [15].

There are various design dimensions of a static analysis fine-tuning its precision (i.e., reduce the false warnings). A data-flow analysis can be *intra-* or *interprocedural*. In the former, effects of a call site on a data-flow are over-approximated, while in the latter, effects are precisely modelled by analyzing the called method(s). Additionally, an interprocedural data-flow analysis is precise if it is *context-sensitive*, which means the data-flow analysis correctly models the call stack and the data-flow returns to the same call site it enters the method. A design dimension for the static analysis of object-oriented languages is *field-sensitivity*. A field-sensitive data-flow analysis reasons precisely with data-flows in the case the data escapes to the heap, i.e., when it is stored within a field of an object and loaded later during execution again.

Apart from being precise, a static analysis is also expected to guarantee *soundness*. For example, a compiler only applies a code optimization if the optimization does not change the program's behavior under *any* given user input. An analysis detecting unchecked null pointer dereferences better finds *all* critical dereferences within the program, a single *false negative*, i.e., if the analysis misses reporting an unchecked flow, may lead to a program crash.

In practice, no static analysis can find all optimizations, all bugs, or all vulnerabilities within a program (no false negatives) and detect those with perfect precision (no false positives). False positives and false negatives are the fundamental consequence of Rice's theorem [35], which states that checking any semantic properties of a program is an undecidable problem. Consequently, any model for static analysis is forced to over- or under-approximate the actual runtime semantics of the program. Over-approximations add false positives to the result and reduce the *precision* of the analysis, while under-approximations introduce false negatives and lower the analysis' *recall*.

Apart from the effect on precision and recall, the approximation is also the influencing factor on the performance of a data-flow analysis. An interprocedural data-flow is less efficient to compute in comparison to an intraprocedural analysis. Adding context- or field-sensitivity to an interprocedural analysis introduces additional complexity within the model and negatively affects the computational effort. Therefore, balancing precision, recall, and performance of a static analysis is a tedious task.

The core contribution of the thesis is a new approach to data-flow analyses that balances precision and performance while retaining the analysis' recall. The solution, called *synchronized pushdown systems* (SPDS), models a context-, field-, and flow-sensitive data-flow analysis taking the form of two pushdown systems [9]. One system models context-sensitivity, and the other one models field-sensitivity. Synchronizing the data-flow results from both systems provides the final results of the data-flow analysis. A context- and field-sensitive analysis is undecidable [32] and forces SPDS to over-approximate. SPDS, though, are specifically designed to expose false positives *only* in corner cases for which the thesis hypothesizes (and confirms in the practical evaluation) that they are virtually non-existent in practice: situations in which an improperly matched caller accesses relevant fields in the same ways as the proper caller would.

2   Motivating Examples

In this section, we show several code flaws that a static data-flow analysis can detect. We highlight *null pointer dereference analysis, taint analysis, typestate analysis* and, an analysis that detects cryptographic misuses. Null pointer dereference analysis is a classical code flaw regularly faced by developers. Taint analysis is primarily used to detect security-related issues such as injection flaws or privacy leaks. Typestate analysis detects misuses of stateful APIs. The research that the thesis presents is fundamental, yet it applies to all these types of data-flow analyses.

2.1 Null Pointer Analysis

Null pointer dereferences cause NullPointerExceptions, one of the most common exception faced by Java developers [18, 26]. A static null pointer analysis detects statements in a program that dereference a potentially uninitialized variable. In Java this typically occurs for fields that are neither initialized nor initialized with null.

```
1  class Car{
2    Engine engine;
3
4    public class Car(){}
5
6    void drive(){
7      //throws a NullPointerException, if called on blueCar.
8      this.engine.start();
9    }
10
11   void setEngine(Engine e){
12     this.engine = e;
13   }
14
15   public static void main(String...args){
16     Car redCar = new Car();
17     redCar.setEngine(new Engine());
18     redCar.drive();
19
20     Car blueCar = new Car();
21     blueCar.drive();
22   }
23 }
```

Fig. 1 An application that crashes in a NullPointerException at runtime in line 8

Figure 1 showcases a program that throws a NullPointerException in line 8 when called from Car::main() in line 21. The program does allocate two Car objects in line 16 and in line 20. For the second object, stored in variable blueCar, no call to setEngine() is present and the field engine remains uninitialized.

Detecting this bug statically is challenging as the analysis needs to be *context-sensitive* to give precise information when the null pointer exception may occur. The analysis needs to distinguish the two objects and the two calling contexts of drive() in line 21 and in line 18. Under the former, the program crashes, whereas under the latter calling context, the program does not crash as setEngine() has priorly been called.

A common approach to model context-sensitivity is the k-limited call-strings approach, which limits the stack of calls by a fixed level of k. In practice, limits of length 1 to 3 are standard to achieve scalable solutions [24, 28]. For object-oriented program, these small values quickly lead to imprecise or unsound results, depending on if the analysis designer choses to over- or under-approximate. SPDS do not require to approximate the call stack.

```
24 class Application{
25   Map<String,String> requestData = new TreeMap<>();
26   Connection conn = ...;
27
28   /** Entry point to the web application.
29    * The HttpServletRequest object contains the payload.
30    */
31   void doGet(HttpServletRequest req, ...){
32     String val = req.getParameter("data"); //Untrusted data
33     Map<String,String> map = this.requestData;
34     map.put("data", val);
35   }
36
37   /** Executes two SQL commands to store this.requestData to the database.
38    */
39   void writeToDatabase(){
40     Map<String,String> map = this.requestData;
41     Statement stmt = this.conn.createStatement();
42     for(Entry<String,String> entry : map.getEntries()){
43       String key = entry.getKey();
44       String value = entry.getValue();
45       String keyQuery = "INSERT INTO keys VALUES (" + key+ ");";
46       stmt.executeQuery(keyQuery);//No SQL injection
47       String keyValueQuery = "INSERT INTO " + key +
48           " VALUES (" + value + ");";
49       stmt.executeQuery(keyValueQuery); //SQL injection
50     }
51   }
52 }
```

Fig. 2 A web application vulnerable to a SQL injection attack

2.2 Taint Analysis

Injection flaws are the most predominant security vulnerabilities in modern software. Injection flaws occur in a program when untrusted data reaches a statement that executes a command (for instance, bash) or when the untrusted data is used to construct a SQL query that is interpreted and executed. In 2017, OWASP[1] lists *Injections* as the top category of vulnerabilities with the highest risk of being exploited. A typical example of an injection attack for a database-backed software system is a *SQL injection*. If a software system contains a SQL-injection vulnerability, the database can be compromised and manipulated, and the system is no longer trustworthy. An attacker can read, add, and even remove data from the database.

A system is vulnerable to a SQL injection attack, if the system does not properly *sanitize* user input and uses the input to execute a dynamically constructed SQL command. Figure 2 demonstrates a minimal back-end of a web application vulnerable to a SQL injection. The back-end maps each incoming request to a call to doGet() within the application and hands over a HttpServletRequest object

---

[1] https://www.owasp.org/.

that represents the request with its parameter. Method `doGet()` loads the user-controllable parameter `"data"` from the request object in line 32 and stores the `String` as value into a `TreeMap`. The `TreeMap` is maintained as field `requestData` of the `Application` object.

Assume the application to persist the map to the database at a later time of execution by calling `writeToDatabase`. The method `writeToDatabase` dereferences the field `this.requestData` to variable `map` in line 40 and iterates over all entries of `map`. For each entry, it constructs and executes two SQL queries (calls in line 46 and in line 49). The first query string only includes a `key` of the map, whereas the second query contains both, the `key` and the `value` of each map's entry. As the `value` of the map contains untrusted data, the application is vulnerable to a SQL injection attack in line 49, which executes the query string contained in variable `keyValueQuery`. With a correct sequence of characters, the attacker can end the SQL insert command and execute any other arbitrary SQL command. For example, a command to delete the whole database.

Static data-flow analysis is an effective technique in preventing such injection flaws. However, detecting the SQL injection flaw in the example by means of a data-flow analysis is challenging to implement efficiently if the analysis is required to be precise and sound at the same time (i.e., no false positive and no false negatives). A precise and sound abstraction for the heap is required to model the data-flow through the map.

Injection flaws are detected by a static *taint analysis*, a special form of data-flow analysis. In the case of a taint analysis for SQL injections, a *taint* is any user-controllable (and hence also attacker-controllable and thus untrusted) input to the program. Starting from these inputs, a taint analysis models program execution and computes other aliased variables that are also *tainted*, i.e., transitively contain the untrusted input. When a tainted variable reaches a SQL query, the analysis reports a *tainted flow*. For the code example in Fig. 2, variable `val` in method `doGet()` is tainted initially. To correctly flag the code as vulnerable, the static taint analysis must model variable `value` in line 44 to be aliased to `val`.

A data-flow analysis trivially detects the alias relationship when the analysis uses an imprecise model. For instance, the *field-insensitive* model taints the whole `TreeMap` object when the tainted variable `val` is added to the `map` in line 34. While field-insensitivity is trivial to model, the analysis results are highly imprecise. Not only are the values of the map tainted, but also any key and the field-insensitive analysis imprecisely marks the constructed SQL query in line 45 as tainted. Therefore, a field-insensitive analysis reports a false positive, as it marks line 46 to execute an unsanitized SQL query.

Field-sensitive data-flow analyses track data-flows through fields of objects and are more precise than field-insensitive analyses. A field-sensitive analysis only reports a single SQL injection for the example. However, the detection of the alias relationship between the variables `value` and `val` is more than non-trivial for a field-sensitive static analysis. The analysis must model the complete data-flow through the map, which spans from the call to `put()` in line 34 to the call in line 44 and involves several accesses to the heap. For instance, at the call to `put()` in line 34,

```
1 public V put(K key, V value) {
2   TreeMap.Entry<K,V> parent = //complex computation done
        earlier
3   TreeMap.Entry<K,V> e = new TreeMap.Entry<>(key, value,
        parent);
4   fixAfterInsertion(e);
5 }
6 private void fixAfterInsertion(Entry<K,V> x) {
7   while (x != null && x != root && x.parent.color == RED) {
8     //removed many branches here...
9     x = parentOf(x);
10     rotateLeft(parentOf(parentOf(x)));
11   }
12 }
13 private void rotateLeft(TreeMap.Entry<K,V> p) {
14   if (p != null) {
15     TreeMap.Entry<K,V> r = p.right;
16     p.right = r.left;
17     if (l.right != null) l.right.parent = p;
18     //removed 8 lines with similar field accesses
19     r.left = p;
20     p.parent = r;
21   }
22 }
```

Listing 1 Excerpt code example of `TreeMap` which is difficult to analyze statically.

the value `val` escapes as second argument to the callee's implementation of the method `put()` of the class `TreeMap`.

Listing 1 shows an excerpt of the callee's code taken from the Java 8 implementation[2] of `TreeMap`. The class contains an inner class `TreeMap.Entry` that lists three fields (`parent`, `right`, and `left`), each of type `TreeMap.Entry`. Method `put()` creates a `TreeMap.Entry` that wraps the inserted element (`value`). The `TreeMap.Entry` is then used to balance the tree (call to `fixAfterInsertion()` in line 56). The method `fixAfterInsertion()` iterates over all `parent` entries and calls `rotateLeft()` to shift around elements within the tree (line 62). The latter method stores to and loads from the fields `parent`, `right`, and `left` of the class `TreeMap.Entry`.

The field-sensitive static taint analysis tracks variable `value`, which is the second parameter of method `put()`. To cope with heap-reachable data-flows, field-sensitive analyses commonly propagate data-flow facts in the form of access paths [1, 2, 4, 5, 6, 10, 14, 41, 42]. An access path comprises a local variable followed

---

[2]http://hg.openjdk.java.net/jdk8/jdk8/jdk/file/eab3c09745b6/src/share/classes/java/util/TreeMap.java.

by a sequence of field accesses, and every field-store statement adds an element to
the sequence. The `while`-loop of `fixAfterInsertion` (line 59) in combination
with the three field stores (lines 68, 71, and 72) within the method `rotateLeft()`
represents a common code pattern[3] that leads to the generation of access paths
of all combinations contained in the set $T = \{\texttt{this}.f_1.f_2.\cdots.f_n.\texttt{value} \mid f_i \in$
$\{\texttt{right}, \texttt{left}, \texttt{parent}\}, n \in \mathbb{N}\}$. The data-flow analysis reports the variable `value`
of method `writeToDatabase()` to alias to variable `val` of method `doGet()` only if
the correct access path exists in the respective set T of the statements retrieving the
value from the map (`getEntries()` in line 42 and `getValue()` in line 44).

The set of data-flow facts T is unbounded. Because most static data-flow
algorithms require a finite data-flow domain, they typically use k-limiting to limit
the field sequence of the access paths to length k [6]. When an access path of
length larger than k is generated, the analysis conservatively over-approximates the
$(k + 1)^{th}$ field. Therefore, not only will the field `value` of a `TreeMap.Entry` of the
map be tainted, but any other field will be tainted as well. For example, any `key`
inserted into the map imprecisely is tainted as `TreeMap.Entry` has a field `key`. For
this particular example, infinitely long field sequences are generated and for any
value of k, k-limiting imprecisely reports `key` to alias to `value`.

Access graphs represent one approach that avoids k-limiting [13, 17]. They
model the "language" of field accesses using an automaton. Access graphs represent
the set T finitely and precisely. However, just as access paths, also access graphs
suffer from the state explosion we show in Listing 1. In the illustrated situation, the
flow-sensitive analysis must store a set similar to T (not necessarily the same) of
data-flow facts, i.e., access graphs, at *every* statement, and potentially *every* context
where a variable pointing to the map exists. Given the large size of T, computing
the data-flow fixed-point for all these statements is highly inefficient, and the use of
access graphs does not improve it.

The thesis presents the solution SPDS that does not suffer from the state
explosion, because a pushdown system efficiently represents millions and even
infinitely many access paths in *one* concise pushdown automaton holding data-flow
results for *all* statements.

2.3 Typestate Analysis

A *typestate analysis* is a static data-flow analysis used, for instance, to detect
misuses of Application Programming Interfaces (APIs) and is capable of detecting
erroneous API uses at compile time, i.e., before execution. Typestate analyses use
an API specification, mostly given in the form of a *finite state machine* (FSM)

---

[3]Recursive data structures, for instance `LinkedList` and `HashMap`, generate such patterns.
Additionally, using inner classes provokes these patterns as the compiler automatically stores the
outer class instance within a field of the inner class.

encoding the intended usage protocol of the API. Based on the specification, the analysis verifies the usage of the API within the code. For example, before an object is destructed, it must be in a state marked as accepting state within the FSM.

The API of the type `java.io.FileWriter` shipped with the standard Java Runtime is a textbook example[4] of an API for which a typestate analysis is helpful in preventing resource leaks. The API can be used to write data from the program to a file on the disk.

To use the API, the developer must first construct a `FileWriter` by supplying a `File` object that the `FileWriter` shall write to. Calling the method `write` on the `FileWriter` object with the respective data as argument tells the `FileWriter` which data shall be written into the `File`. Writing the content of a file to disk is an expensive operation delegated to the operation system, and the API delays the respective system calls to the `close()` method of the `FileWriter` object. The API assumes the `close()` method to be called exactly once prior to the destruction of the object. If the user of the API does not call `close()`, the file remains open. The file resource is blocked by the process, and other processes may not read and write the same file and the program has a *resource leak*. Additionally, data is never written to the file as the output is only flushed to the file upon calling `close()`.

Figure 3 shows the finite state machine that represents a correct usage pattern for the API. The state labeled by I is the initial state. The transition into this state is labeled by `<init>` and refers to the constructor of a `FileWriter` object. The accepting states are the states I and C, the latter is the state in which the `FileWriter` object is correctly closed. All transitions into the C state are labeled by `close`. The state machine lists a third state (W) that the object switches into after a `write` call. In this state, data has been written to the `FileWriter` object but not yet persisted to the actual file on disk. Therefore, it is not an accepting state.

Fig. 3 The API usage pattern encoded as finite state machine for the class `java.io.FileWriter`

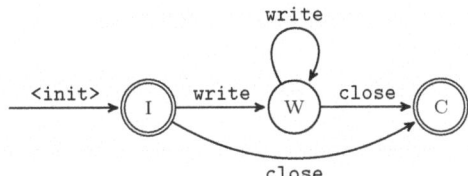

The program in Fig. 4 shows a code snippet that uses the API. The code constructs a `FileWriter` object and stores it into field `writer` of the `Example` object. After method `bar()` is called, the field `writer` is loaded and the contained `FileWriter` object is `closed` in line 81.

One challenge of a typestate analysis is to perform *strong updates* when the state of an object changes. At the `close()` call in line 81, it is not clear which actual

---

[4]In Java 7, `try-with-resources` blocks were introduced to automatically `close` and release file handles. We assume the developer does not use these syntax elements.

Fig. 4 Simple, but
challenging program to
analysis for a typestate
analysis

```
75 class Example{
76   FileWriter writer;
77   public void foo() throws IOException {
78     File file = new File("Data.txt");
79     this.writer = new FileWriter(file);
80     bar();
81     this.writer.close();
82   }
83 }
```

object is closed. If method bar() allocates a new FileWriter and overwrites the field writer, the FileWriter allocated in line 79 remains open and the typestate analysis cannot strongly update the state of the latter object. If the analysis detects only a single object to ever be pointed to by field writer at statement 81, a strong update can be made. However, the typestate analysis suddenly requires precise points-to information, which is notoriously challenging to obtain efficiently.

Points-to analysis computes points-to information. Despite much prior effort, it is known that a precise points-to analysis does not scale for the whole program [25]. Instead, the typestate analysis only requires points-to information for a rather small subset of all pointer variables, namely the variables pointing to objects that the FileWriter is stored within.

The thesis presents BOOMERANG, a demand-driven, and hence efficient, points-to analysis that computes results for a query given in the form of a pointer variable at a statement. BOOMERANG is precise (context-, flow-, and field-sensitive). Based on BOOMERANG, the thesis presents the data-flow framework IDE^{al}, a framework that is powerful enough to encode a typestate analysis that performs strong updates.

2.4 Cryptographic Misuses

Almost any software system processes, stores, or interacts with sensitive data. Such data typically includes user credentials in the form of e-mail addresses and passwords, as well as company data such as the company's income, employee's health, and medical data. Cryptography is the field of computer science that develops solutions to protect the privacy of data and to avoid malicious tampering.

Software developers should have a basic understanding of key concepts in cryptography to build secure software systems. Prior studies [8, 30] have shown that software developers commonly struggle to do so and as a result fail to implement cryptographic[5] tasks securely. While cryptography is a complex and difficult-to-understand area, it also evolves quickly and software developers must continuously remain informed about broken and out-dated cryptographic algorithms and configurations.

---

[5]Hereafter, used interchangeably with crypto.

```
 84  public class Encrypter{
 85    private SecretKey key;
 86    private int keyLength = 448;
 87
 88    public Encrypter(){
 89      KeyGenerator keygen = KeyGenerator.getInstance("Blowfish");
 90      keygen.init(this.keyLength);
 91      this.key = keygen.generateKey();
 92    }
 93
 94    public byte[] encrypt(String plainText){
 95      Cipher cipher = Cipher.getInstance("AES");
 96      //cipher.init(Cipher.ENCRYPT_MODE, this.key);
 97      byte[] encText = cipher.doFinal(plainText.getBytes());
 98      return encText;
 99    }
100  }
```

Fig. 5 An example of a misuse of a cryptographic API

But it is not only the lack of education on the developer's side, common crypto APIs are also difficult to use correctly and securely. For instance, implementing a data encryption with the Java Cryptographic Architecture[6] (JCA), the standard crypto API in Java, requires the developer to combine multiple low-level crypto tasks such as secure key generation, choosing between symmetric or asymmetric crypto algorithms in combination with matching block schemes and padding modes. While the JCA design is flexible to accommodate any potential combination, it yields to developers implementing crypto tasks insecurely by misusing the API.

Figure 5 demonstrates an example code that incorrectly uses some of the JCA's classes for encryption. At instantiation time of an Encrypter object, the constructor generates a SecretKey for algorithm "Blowfish" (parameter to the call to getInstance() in line 89) of size 448 (parameter to call in line 90). In line 91, the key is stored to field key of the constructed Encrypter instance. The Encrypter object's public API offers a method encrypt(), which, when called, creates a Cipher object in line 95. The Cipher object is configured to encrypt data using the "AES" algorithm (parameter to the call to getInstance() in line 95). The developer commented out line 96 that (1) initializes the algorithm's mode and (2) passes the SecretKey stored in field key to the Cipher object. The call to doFinal() in line 97 performs the encryption operation and encrypts the content of the plainText and stores it in the byte array encText.

There are four API misuses in this code example. First, the developer commented-out a required call in line 96. Second, if the developer includes the line in the comment, the generated key ("Blowfish") and the encryption cipher ("AES") do not match. Third, and related, the key length of 448 is not suitable for the algorithm AES that expects a size of 128, 192, or 256. Fourth, depending on the

---

[6]https://docs.oracle.com/javase/8/docs/technotes/guides/security/crypto/CryptoSpec.html.

crypto provider, AES is used with electronic codebook (ECB) mode. Using ECB results in low entropy within the bytes of encText. The first three API misuses throw exceptions at runtime that, using static analysis, could already be detected at compile time. Using ECB, however, does not throw an exception and silently leads to insecure code.

Such API misuses are found in real-world software artifacts. To cope with the detection of such misuses, in [20], we present a domain-specific language (DSL), called CrySL, for the specification of API usage *rules*. We designed a static analysis compiler that, based on a set of CrySL rules, automatically generates a static analysis. The analysis uses BOOMERANG and IDE^{al} and hereby is able to detect misuses even across data-flow constructs such as fields and callings contexts of distinct objects.

3 Synchronized Pushdown Systems

Pushdown systems solve context-free language reachability and have been studied intensively [3, 9, 21, 23, 34]. Synchronized Pushdown Systems (SPDS) [39] are one of the core contributions of the dissertation.

SPDS combines two pushdown systems, the pushdown system of calls and the fields-pushdown system. For each pushdown system, SPDS builds on existing efficient algorithms. When both pushdown systems are synchronized, the results yield a highly precise context- and field-sensitive data-flow analysis.

3.1 Calls-Pushdown System

The calls-pushdown system models the data-flow along the use-def chains of variables and also models the data-flow of variables along call and return methods.

Definition 1 A *pushdown system* is a triple $\mathcal{P} = (P, \Gamma, \Delta)$, where P and Γ are finite sets called the *control locations* and the *stack alphabet*, respectively. A *configuration* is a pair $\langle\!\langle p, w \rangle\!\rangle$, where $p \in P$ and $w \in \Gamma^*$, i.e., a control location with a sequence of stack elements. The finite set Δ is composed of *rules*. A rule has the form $\langle\!\langle p, \gamma \rangle\!\rangle \to \langle\!\langle p', w \rangle\!\rangle$, where $p, p' \in P$, $\gamma \in \Gamma$, and $w \in \Gamma^*$. The length of w determines the type of the rule. A rule with $|w| = 1$ is called a *normal rule*, one with length 2 a *push rule*, and a rule of length 0 a *pop rule*. If the length of w is larger than 2, the rule can be decomposed into multiple push rules of length 2.

The rules of a pushdown system $\mathcal{P}$ define a relation $\Rightarrow$: If there exists a rule $\langle\!\langle p, \gamma \rangle\!\rangle \to \langle\!\langle p', w \rangle\!\rangle$, then $\langle\!\langle p, \gamma w' \rangle\!\rangle \Rightarrow \langle\!\langle p', ww' \rangle\!\rangle$ for all $w' \in \Gamma^*$. Based on an initial start configuration c, the transitive closure of the relation ($\Rightarrow^*$) defines a set of reachable configuration $post^*(c) = \{c' \mid c \Rightarrow^* c'\}$. The set $post^*(c)$ is infinite

```
                                              106  foo(A a){              a   b
101  main(){                    u   v   w     107    if(...){
102    A u = new A();                         108      return a;
103    A v = u;                               109    }
104    A w = foo(v);                          110    b = foo(a);
105  }                                        111    return b;
                                              112  }
```

⟶ Normal rule of $\mathcal{P}_\mathbb{S}$ ⤳ Transitive Data-Flow

Fig. 6 Example of the data-flow within a recursive program

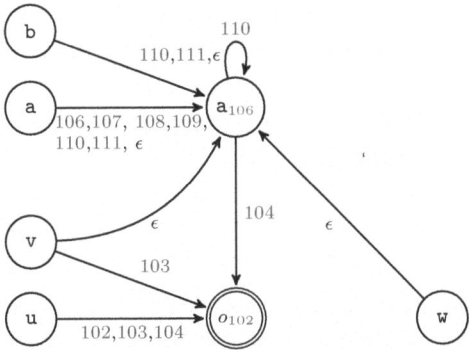

Fig. 7 The automat $\mathcal{A}_\mathbb{S}$ after saturation based on $\mathcal{P}_\mathbb{S}$

but has a finite representation in the form of an automaton. The algorithm post*
constructs this automaton based on a given pushdown system.

Example 1 Figure 6 shows a program that instantiates an object (o_{102}). The object
is stored and loaded to and from the local variables u and v. The variable v is used
as argument to the call in 104. Next to the program, a directed graph represents the
rules of the pushdown system of calls (hereafter $\mathcal{P}_\mathbb{S}$). Each edge represents a normal
rule of $\mathcal{P}_\mathbb{S}$. Additionally, the pushdown system contains the push rule $\langle\!\langle v, 103 \rangle\!\rangle \rightarrow$
$\langle\!\langle a, 106 \cdot 104 \rangle\!\rangle$ and the pop rule $\langle\!\langle b, 111 \rangle\!\rangle \rightarrow \langle\!\langle w, \epsilon \rangle\!\rangle$.

Based on the pushdown system $\mathcal{P}_\mathbb{S}$ and given an initial automaton accepting u at
102, the post* algorithms construct an automaton that encodes the reachability of the
object o_{102}. Figure 7 depicts the saturated automaton that encodes the reachability
of the object o_{102}.

The automaton also encodes the calling context under which each variable
reaches (or points-to) the initial object. For instance, variable a in line 110 points
to o_{102} under call stack 104. The program is recursive and there are potentially
infinitely many calls on the call stack. Accordingly, the automaton contains a loop
labeled by 110.

3.2 Field-Pushdown System

The call-pushdown system models the calling contexts and its context-sensitivity; however, it is designed field-insensitively and over-approximates access to fields.

Field store and load statements can also be modelled precisely as a pushdown system. Hereby, a field store statement matches a push rule, and a load statement resembles a pop rule. The fields-pushdown system overcomes the imprecision of k-limiting and renders the analysis more efficient.

k-limited analyses with low values of k, e.g., $k = 1, 2, 3$, are efficient to compute but quickly introduce imprecision into the results; higher values of k make the analysis precise but also affect the analysis time exponentially. In our practical evaluation, we compare our abstraction to k-limiting and show that pushdown systems are as efficient as $k = 1$ while being as precise as $k = \infty$ [37].

Definition 2 The *field-PDS* is the pushdown system $\mathcal{P}_\mathbb{F} = (\mathbb{V} \times \mathbb{S}, \mathbb{F} \cup \{\epsilon\}, \Delta_\mathbb{F})$. A control location of this system is a pair of a variable and a statement. We use $x@s$ for an element $(x, s) \in \mathbb{V} \times \mathbb{S}$. The notation emphasizes that fact x holds *at* statement s. The pushdown system pushes and pops elements of $\mathbb{F}$ to and from the stack. An empty stack is represented by the ϵ field.

We write a configuration of $\mathcal{P}_\mathbb{F}$ as $\langle\!\langle x@s, f_0 \cdot f_1 \cdot \ldots f_n \rangle\!\rangle$. The configuration reads as follows: The data-flow at statement s is accessible via the access path $x.f_0 \cdot f_1 \cdot \ldots f_n$.

$\mathcal{P}_\mathbb{S}$ and $\mathcal{P}_\mathbb{F}$ have similar set of rules. The major differences are at field store and load statements. A field store generates a push rule, a field load statement a pop rule.

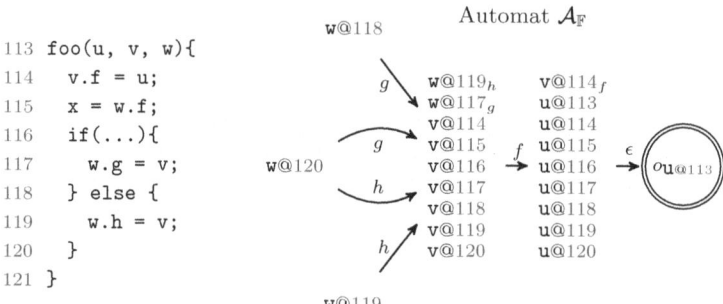

Fig. 8 Example code and $\mathcal{A}_\mathbb{F}$ automaton. The automaton $\mathcal{A}_\mathbb{F}$ is constructed based on the initial configuration $\langle\!\langle u@114, \epsilon \rangle\!\rangle$ and saturated based on the rules provided in Table 1

Example 2 Figure 8 depicts a program code containing three field stores and one field load statement. Table 1 lists the push and pop rules of $\mathcal{P}_\mathbb{F}$. Given the initial configuration $\langle\!\langle u@114, \epsilon \rangle\!\rangle$, algorithm post* computes the automaton given in Fig. 8. This automaton contains field- and flow-sensitive data-flow results. For instance, the automaton encodes that the object initially contained in variable u is also reachable

Table 1 Push and pop rules contained in $\Delta_{\mathbb{F}}$ of $\mathcal{P}_{\mathbb{F}}$ for the program code in Fig. 8. The wildcard ($*$) of the push rules represents a rule for any $g \in \mathbb{F}$

Push Rules		
$\langle\!\langle \text{u@}113, * \rangle\!\rangle \rightarrow \langle\!\langle \text{v@}114, \text{f} \cdot * \rangle\!\rangle$		
$\langle\!\langle \text{v@}116, * \rangle\!\rangle \rightarrow \langle\!\langle \text{w@}117, \text{g} \cdot * \rangle\!\rangle$	Pop Rules	
$\langle\!\langle \text{v@}118, * \rangle\!\rangle \rightarrow \langle\!\langle \text{w@}119, \text{h} \cdot * \rangle\!\rangle$	$\langle\!\langle \text{w@}114, \text{f} \rangle\!\rangle \rightarrow \langle\!\langle \text{w@}115, \epsilon \rangle\!\rangle$	

via `w.g.f` and `w.h.f`. The automaton does not contain a node that references `x`, which means variable `x` of the program does not point to the same object as `u`.

3.3 Synchronization of Call-PDS and Field-PDS

While the call-pushdown system is field-*in*sensitive, the field-pushdown system is context-*in*sensitive. Synchronized pushdown systems overcome the weaknesses of each system and yield context- and field-sensitive data-flow results. The key idea is to synchronize the results of the saturated post* automaton of both pushdown systems. Note, the synchronization is *not* an automaton intersection. Both automata use different stack alphabets and encode different languages.

Definition 3 For the call-PDS $\mathcal{P}_{\mathbb{S}} = (\mathbb{V}, \mathbb{S}, \Delta_{\mathbb{S}})$ and the field-PDS $\mathcal{P}_{\mathbb{F}} = (\mathbb{V} \times \mathbb{S}, \mathbb{F} \cup \{\epsilon\}, \Delta_{\mathbb{F}})$, the *synchronized pushdown systems* are the quintuple SPDS $= (\mathbb{V}, \mathbb{S}, \mathbb{F} \cup \{\epsilon\}, \Delta_{\mathbb{F}}, \Delta_{\mathbb{S}})$. A configuration of SPDS extends from the configuration of each system: A *synchronized configuration* is a triple $(v, s, f) \in \mathbb{V} \times \mathbb{S}^+ \times \mathbb{F}^*$, which we denote as $\langle\!\langle v.f_1 \cdot \ldots \cdot f_m @ s_0^{s_1 \ldots s_n} \rangle\!\rangle$ where $s = s_0 \cdot s_1 \cdot \ldots \cdot s_n$ and $f = f_1 \cdot \ldots \cdot f_m$. For synchronized pushdown systems, we define the set of all reachable synchronized configurations from a start configuration $c = \langle\!\langle v.f_1 \cdot \ldots \cdot f_m @ s_0^{s_1 \ldots s_n} \rangle\!\rangle$ to be

$$post_{\text{SF}}(c) = \{\langle\!\langle w.g @ t_0^{t_1 \ldots t_n} \rangle\!\rangle \mid \langle\!\langle w @ t_0, g \rangle\!\rangle \in post_{\mathbb{F}}^*(\langle\!\langle v @ s_0, f \rangle\!\rangle)$$

$$\wedge \langle\!\langle w, t \rangle\!\rangle \in post_{\mathbb{S}}^*(\langle\!\langle v, s \rangle\!\rangle)\}. \tag{1}$$

Hence, a synchronized configuration c is accepted if $\langle\!\langle v, s_0 \cdot \ldots \cdot s_n \rangle\!\rangle \in \mathcal{A}_{\mathbb{S}}$ and $\langle\!\langle v @ s_0, f_1 \cdot \ldots \cdot f_m \rangle\!\rangle \in \mathcal{A}_{\mathbb{F}}$, and $post_{\text{SF}}(c)$ can be represented by the automaton pair $(\mathcal{A}_{\mathbb{S}}, \mathcal{A}_{\mathbb{F}})$, which we refer to as $\mathcal{A}_{\mathbb{S}}^{\mathbb{F}}$.

Intuitively, a configuration SPDS is accepted, only if the field automaton *and* the call automaton accept the configuration.

Example 3 Figure 9 shows an example of a program with a data-flow path of interwined calling context and field accesses. A directed graph below the code visualizes the data-flow. Vertical edges correspond to calling context (push rules $\hat{=}$ opening parentheses / pop rule $\hat{=}$ closing parentheses), while horizontal edges

Fig. 9 A code example for
and a representation of the
code as directed graph

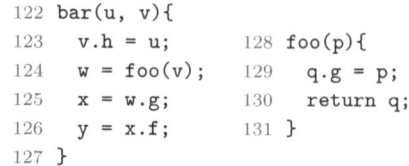

```
122 bar(u, v){
123    v.h = u;          128 foo(p){
124    w = foo(v);       129    q.g = p;
125    x = w.g;          130    return q;
126    y = x.f;          131 }
127 }
```

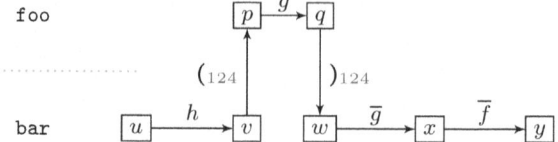

correspond to field store and loads. A field label with a line on top, e.g., $\overline{f}$, means the field f is loaded. SPDS computes reachability within this graph.[7] For the program, SPDS computes variable $\underline{y}$ *not* to point to u@122. The word along the path from $\underline{y}$ to u is $h \cdot (_{124} \cdot g \cdot)_{124} \cdot \overline{g} \cdot \overline{f}$.

The parentheses $(_{124}$ and $)_{124}$ are properly matched in the context-free language, and the path is context-sensitively feasible. However, the path is not feasible in a field-sensitive manner. The field store access g matches the field load access $\overline{g}$, however, the field store of h does not match the field load $\overline{f}$.

Any context- and field-sensitive data-flow analysis is undecidable [32]. Therefore, also SPDS must over-approximate. Indeed, it is possible to construct cases in which the analysis returns imprecise results [37]. In the evaluation however, we were not able to find such cases in practice.

4 Boomerang

A points-to set is a set of abstract objects (e.g., allocation statements) that a variable may point-to at runtime. SPDS does *not* compute full points-to set, but only a subset of the points-to set of a variable. Points-to analysis is a non-distributive problem [33, 40], SPDS, however, propagates distributive information and (intentionally) under-approximates the points-to set of a variable. Field accesses allow indirect data-flows that are non-distributive. BOOMERANG is a pointer analysis that builds on top of SPDS and computes points-to and all alias sets. All parts that can be computed in a distributive fashion using SPDS, non-distributive parts are handled as an additional fixed point computation. BOOMERANG is demand driven and answers queries. A query is a variable at a statement that BOOMERANG computes the points-to set for. For each query, BOOMERANG carefully combines forward- and backward-directed

---

[7]SPDS computes the reachability within the two automata $\mathcal{A}_{\mathbb{S}}$ and $\mathcal{A}_{\mathbb{F}}$. To keep the visualization simple, the automata are omitted.

```
132  foo(){
133      u = new;
134      v = u;
135      x = new;
136      u.f = x;
137      y = v.f;
138  }
```

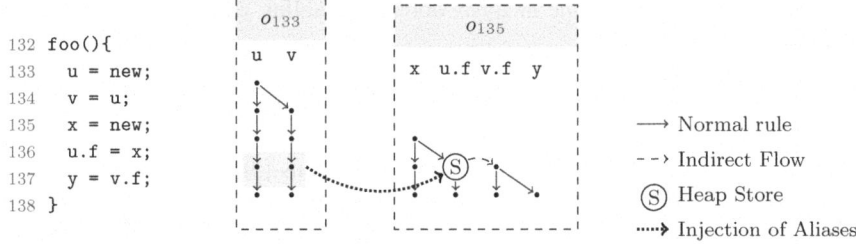

$\longrightarrow$ Normal rule

$- -$› Indirect Flow

Ⓢ Heap Store

$\cdots\cdots$➤ Injection of Aliases

Fig. 10 Non-distributivity of pointer relations

data-flow analyses and focuses on the minimal program slice necessary to answer each query.

Example 4 Figure 10 is a minimal example showing that pointer relations are non-distributive. The program instantiates two objects o_{133} and o_{135} in lines 133 and 135. During runtime x and y both variable point to the object o_{135}. The object is stored to access path u.f in line 135, which at runtime, also changes the content of access path v.f as u and v alias. Using only a single SPDS, the static analysis only propagates the data-flow in line 135 from x to u.f but not to v.f. Therefore, a SPDS does not deliver sound points-to information. BOOMERANG, however, instantiates one SPDS per object allocation and uses an additional fixed-point iteration to connect indirect data-flows across multiple SPDS. Figure 10 indicates such indirect data-flow in form of the blue dashed arrow.

A single program frequently allocates several thousand of objects, and computing data-flow for each of those object does not scale if the analysis is field- and context-sensitive. Instead of starting at every allocation site, BOOMERANG uses a demand-driven design. A backward analysis decides which object allocation is relevant for a single forward query [40].

5   Typestate Analyses Based on IDE^{al}

With IDE^{al} the dissertation further extends SPDS and BOOMERANG. IDE^{al} is a general framework for data-flow analysis and can be used for typestate analysis or API usage mining. IDE^{al} lifts $\mathcal{P}_{\mathbb{S}}$ and associated a weight to each rule. The new idea of IDE^{al} is to use weights to carry additional information along each data-flow path, for instance, to encode typestate information as motivated in Sect. 2.3.

For a typestate analysis, the weights carry the actual state the object resides in at every program point. Previous research on typestate analysis [11, 12] encoded the state of the object as additional information within the data-flow domain, which unnecessarily increases the state space of the analysis and leads to state explosion. With weights, IDE^{al} separates alias information from typestate information and reduces the state space of the analysis domain, enabling additional performance benefits.

As motivated in Sect. 2.3, in the case of typestate, also aliasing of variables plays an important role and IDE^{al} resorts to BOOMERANG to trigger on-demand queries to perform strong updates of the states [38].

In several experiments presented within publications [38, 39] as well as in the dissertation [37], we compare an IDE^{al}-based typestate analysis to a state-of-the-art typestate analysis, we show that the new concept of separating alias information and weights for typestate yields additional performance benefits.

6 CogniCrypt

BOOMERANG, IDE^{al}, and SPDS also form the base technology behind the static analysis component of the tool CogniCrypt.[8] CogniCrypt is an Eclipse plugin and is part of CROSSING, an interdisciplinary collaborative research center at the Technical University of Darmstadt. CogniCrypt supports software developers in correctly using cryptographic APIs within their software implementations. CogniCrypt accepts rules as input and automatically compiles them into an IDE^{al}- and BOOMERANG-based static analysis. The rules are written in a new domain-specific language, called CrySL.

6.1 The CrySL Language

To detect such API misuses, Krüger et al. [20] designed CrySL, a domain-specific language that allows the specification of crypto API uses. CrySL defines a whitelist approach that specifies correct uses of an API. *CryptoAnalysis* is the component that compiles a set of rules to a static analysis. Executing the static analysis on program code reports parts of the code that deviate from the specification. We briefly introduce the main semantics of the language in this section and discuss the basic design of *CryptoAnalysis*. The language definition and CrySL rule specifications[9] are not part of the dissertation.

With the CrySL specifications for the JCA, *CryptoAnalysis* is able to detect all four crypto-related issues showcased in Fig. 5. We discuss the important syntax elements of CrySL based on a minimal[10] CrySL specification covering the misuses in Fig. 5. We refer to the original work [20] for the definition of all syntax elements of CrySL.

---

[8]https://www.eclipse.org/cognicrypt/.

[9]https://github.com/CROSSINGTUD/Crypto-API-Rules.

[10]The complete specification is found at https://github.com/CROSSINGTUD/Crypto-API-Rules.

```
141 SPEC javax.crypto.KeyGenerator
142 OBJECTS
143   int keySize;
144   javax.crypto.SecretKey key;
145   java.lang.String algorithm;
146 EVENTS
147   Get: getInstance(algorithm);
148   Inits: init(keySize);
149   GenerateKey: key = generateKey();
150 ORDER
151   Gets, Inits, GenerateKey
152 CONSTRAINTS
153   algorithm in {"AES", "Blowfish", ...};
154   keySize in {128, 192, 256};
155 ENSURES
156   generatedKey[key, algorithm];
```

(a)

```
157 SPEC  javax.crypto.Cipher
158 OBJECTS
159   java.lang.String trans;
160   byte[] plainText;
161   java.security.Key key;
162   byte[] cipherText;
163 EVENTS
164   Get: getInstance(trans);
165   Init: init(_, key);
166   doFinal: cipherText = doFinal(plainText);
167 ORDER
168   Get, Init, (doFinal)+
169 CONSTRAINTS
170   part(0, "/", trans) in {"AES", "Blowfish", "DESede", ..., "RSA"};
171   part(0, "/", trans) in {"AES"} => part(1, "/", trans) in {"CBC"};
172 REQUIRES
173   generatedKey[key, part(0, "/", trans)];
174 ENSURES
175   encrypted[cipherText, plainText];
```

(b)

Fig. 11 Two simplified CrySL rules for the JCA. (a) CrySL rule for javax.crypto.KeyGenerator. (b) CrySL rule for javax.crypto.Cipher

A CrySL specification is comprised of multiple CrySL *rules*. Each CrySL rule starts with **SPEC** clause specifying the type of the class that the CrySL rule is defined for. Figure 11 depicts two CrySL rules for the classes javax.crypto.Cipher and javax.crypto.KeyGenerator. The **SPEC** clause is followed by an **OBJECTS** block that defines a set of *rule members*. The values of the rule members are then constrained on within the **CONSTRAINTS** block. For instance, the **CONSTRAINTS** for the rule to KeyGenerator restricts the rule member keySize in line 154 to the values 128, 192, or 256. When using a KeyGenerator, the integer value for keySize must be one of the listed values.

The **EVENTS** block defines labels (e.g., Get in line 147 and Inits in line 148), each label is a set of events. An event is an invocation of a method and is defined via the method signature. For example, label Inits is defined as the event of calling the method with signature init(int keySize) (line 148). The parameter name (keySize) matches the name of a rule member, and when the program calls the event's method, the value of the parameter of the call is bound to the rule member keySize, which means that the parameter must satisfy the given constraint.

The labels defined within the **EVENTS** block are used in the **ORDER** block. The **ORDER** clause lists a regular expression (inducing a finite state machine) over the labels and defines the usage pattern (i.e., typestate property) of the specified type. Each object of the specification is required to follow the defined usage pattern. For instance, the specification for KeyGenerator expects each object of its type to call any method of the label GetInstance prior to any of the Inits call followed by a GenerateKey call. The **ORDER** specification for Cipher uses a + for the label doFinal, indicating that the method doFinal() must be called at least once and arbitrary additional calls of the method can follow.

The remaining two blocks are the **REQUIRES** and **ENSURES** block of a rule. Each line of these blocks lists a *predicate*. A predicate is defined by a name followed by a list of parameters. CrySL predicates cover the specification of the interaction of multiple objects of different types. The KeyGenerator rule lists a predicate generatedKey with two parameters key and algorithm in the **ENSURES** block in line 156. When an object of type KeyGenerator is used according to the specification in the **CONSTRAINTS**, **ORDER**, and **REQUIRES** block, the predicate listed in the **ENSURES** block is generated for the object. Other CrySL rules that interact with KeyGenerator objects can list the predicate in their **REQUIRES** block. For instance, the CrySL rule Cipher lists the predicate generatedKey as a required predicate in line 173.

6.2   Compiling CrySL to a Static Analysis

CryptoAnalysis is a static analysis compiler that transforms CrySL rules into a static analysis. Internally, *CryptoAnalysis* is composed of three static sub-analyses: (1) an IDE^{al}-based typestate analysis, (2) a BOOMERANG instance with extensions to extract String and int parameters on-the-fly and (3) an IDE^{al}-based taint analysis (i.e., all weights are identity). The three static analyses deliver input to a constraint solver that warns if any part of the CrySL specification is violated.

Example 5 We discuss a walk-through of *CryptoAnalysis* based on the CrySL specification defined in Fig. 11, and the code snippet provided in Fig. 5. *CryptoAnalysis* first constructs a call graph and computes call-graph reachable allocation sites for in CrySL-specified types. Factory methods can also serve as allocation sites. For example, the factory methods getInstance() of Cipher and KeyGenerator internally create objects of the respective type, and *CryptoAnalysis* considers these calls as allocations sites. In the code example in Fig. 5 the allocation sites are the objects o_{89} and o_{95}.

Starting at the allocation sites, *CryptoAnalysis* uses IDE^{al} to check if the object satisfies the **ORDER** clause of the rule. The call sequence on the KeyGenerator object o_{89} satisfies the required typestate automaton defined as regular expression in the **ORDER** block. Opposed to that, the Cipher object o_{95} does not satisfy the **ORDER** clause, because the developer commented out line 96. *CryptoAnalysis* warns the developer about the violation of this clause (line 168).

CryptoAnalysis also extracts String and int parameters of events (statements that change the typestate) to bind the actual values to the rule members of a CrySL rule. For instance, the getInstance("Blowfish") call in line 89 binds the value "Blowfish" to the rule member algorithm of the CrySL rule for KeyGenerator. In this example, the String value is easy to extract statically, but it might also be defined elsewhere in the program. For example, the value binding for the rule member keySize is the actual int value flowing to the init call in line 90 as a parameter. The actual value is loaded from the heap, because it is the value of the instance field keyLength of the Encrypter object. Therefore, *CryptoAnalysis* triggers a BOOMERANG query for 90 to find the actual int value of the field.

To conclude, *CryptoAnalysis* infers that object o_{89} generates a SecretKey for the algorithm "Blowfish" with a key length of 448 in line 91. The KeyGenerator rule disallows the chosen key length (**CONSTRAINTS** in line 154), and *CryptoAnalysis* warns the developer to choose an appropriate keySize.

Assume the developer to change the code to use an appropriate value for keySize, and the KeyGenerator is used in compliance to its CrySL specification, then *CryptoAnalysis* generates the predicate generatedKey for the SecretKey object stored to field key of the Encrypter instance as expected.

If, additionally, the developer includes the init call on the cipher object in line 96, (1) the **ORDER** clause of the CrySL rule for Cipher is satisfied and (2) the generatedKey predicate flows via the field this.key to the Cipher object o_{95}. As the Cipher rule **REQUIRES** the predicate (line 173), the **ORDER** and **REQUIRES** blocks for the object o_{95} are satisfied.

However, the **CONSTRAINTS** for object o_{95} are still not satisfied. Therefore, *CryptoAnalysis* reports that (1) the key is generated for algorithm "Blowfish", and this selection does not fit the algorithm chosen for Cipher ("AES") and (2) when using algorithm "AES", one should use it in "CBC" mode (**CONSTRAINTS** in

line 171). When the developer fixes these two mistakes, *CryptoAnalysis* reports
the code to correctly use the JCA with respect to the CrySL rule.

6.3   Evaluation on Maven Central

Maven Central is the most popular software repository to which developers can
publish their software artifacts. Publishing allows other developers to easily access
and include the software into their own projects. At the time the experiment was
conducted, over 2.7 million software artifacts were published at Maven Central.

The repository contains artifacts in different versions. For one experiment of the
thesis, we run *CryptoAnalysis* on all artifacts in their latest versions of Maven
Central, a total of 152.996 artifacts. For over 85.7% of all crypto-using Maven
artifacts, the analysis terminates in under 10 min, and on average each analysis
takes 88 s. Given that *CryptoAnalysis* performs a highly precise and sophisticated
static analysis, these results are promising. Unfortunately, we also discovered that
many artifacts use the JCA insecurely, and 68.7% of all crypto-using Maven artifacts
contain at least one misuse.

Example 6 We want to elaborate on one finding more closely, because it shows the
capability of the analysis. Listing 2 shows a code excerpt of an artifact that uses a
`KeyStore` object. A `KeyStore` stores certificates and is protected with a password.
A `KeyStore` object has a method `load()` whose second parameter is a password.
The API expects the password to be handed over as a `char[]` array. The `KeyStore`
API explicitly uses the primitive type instead of a `String`, because `String`s are
immutable and cannot be cleared.[11] However, many implementations convert the
password from a `String` and hereby introduce a security vulnerability; when not
yet garbage collected, the actual password can be extracted from memory, e.g., via
a memory dump.

CryptoAnalysis detects the two security vulnerabilities code presented in
Listing 2. First, the password is converted from a `String` object via a call to
`toCharArray()` to the actual array (line 199), i.e., during the execution of the code
the password is maintained in memory as `String`. Second, under some conditions
(lines 178, 182, and 189 must evaluate to *true*), the password is hard-coded.

CryptoAnalysis reports a **CONSTRAINTS** error on this example, because the
`String pass` (highlighted by the green box) in line 199 may contain the `String`
`"changeit"` as it is defined in line 179 (also highlighted). The data-flow corresponding to the finding is non-trivial to detect manually; however, *CryptoAnalysis*
is able to do so by the support of BOOMERANG. *CryptoAnalysis* triggers a
BOOMERANG query for the second parameter of the `load()` call in line 199 and
finds the `toCharArray()` call. From that call, the analysis traces the variable `pass`

---

[11]https://docs.oracle.com/javase/7/docs/technotes/guides/security/crypto/CryptoSpec.html#
PBEEx.

```
23 protected String getKeystorePassword(){
24   String keyPass = (String)this.attributes.get("keypass");
25   if (keyPass == null) {
26     keyPass = "changeit";
27   }
28   String keystorePass = (String)this.attributes.get("
         keystorePass");
29   if (keystorePass == null) {
30     keystorePass = keyPass;
31   }
32   return keystorePass;
33 }
34 protected KeyStore getTrustStore(){
35   String truststorePassword = getKeystorePassword();
36   if (truststorePassword != null) {
37     ts = getStore(..., ..., truststorePassword);
38   }
39   return ts;
40 }
41 private KeyStore getStore(String type, String path, String
         pass){
42   KeyStore ks = KeyStore.getInstance(type);
43   if ((!"PKCS11".equalsIgnoreCase(type)) && ...){
44     ...
45   }
46   ks.load(istream, pass .toCharArray());
47   return ks;
48 }
```

Listing 2 Simplified real-world code example with a hard-coded password

in method getStore() and finds it to be a parameter of getStore(), and the data-flow propagation continues at invocations of the method. The method getStore() is called in line 190, where BOOMERANG data-flow propagation follows the variable truststorePassword. This variable is assigned the return value of the call site in line 188. The backward data-flow analysis continues in line 185 and eventually finds the allocation site "changeit" in the highlighted line with the line number 179. Eventually, *CryptoAnalysis* reports that variable pass is of type String and that it may contain the hard-coded password "changeit".

7 Conclusion

Finding an acceptable balance between precision, recall, and performance of a static analysis is a tedious task when designing and implementing a static analysis. With SPDS, BOOMERANG, and IDE^{al}, the dissertation presents new approaches to static data-flow analysis that is demand-driven context-, field-, and flow-sensitive, or in short precise and efficient.

In this chapter, we first motivate (Sect. 2) various applications ranging from null pointer analysis to typestate analysis and next detail on the contributions SPDS, BOOMERANG, and IDE^{al}.

With SPDS (Sect. 3), we present a precise and efficient solution to a known to be undecidable problem [32]. SPDS synchronizes the results of two pushdown systems, one that models field-sensitivity, and a second that models context-sensitivity. SPDS presents a theoretical as well a practical new model to data-flow analysis. The new formal approach to data-flow analysis also enables a direction for future work, for instance, to additionally summarize the pushdown systems [22].

The demand-driven pointer analysis BOOMERANG, presented in Sect. 4, addresses pointer analysis, which is known to be hard to scale. BOOMERANG gains efficiency as it separates the distributive parts of a non-distributive propagation into efficiently SPDS-solvable sub-problems.

IDE^{al} (Sect. 5) extends the ideas of the distributive propagations of BOOMERANG and additionally propagates weights along the data-flow path. The weights allow data-flow analyses to model typestate analyses. In an experiment presented within the dissertation, we compare an IDE^{al}-based typestate analysis to a state-of-the-art typestate analysis and show the efficiency benefit of distributive propagation.

Lastly, we showcase the application of SPDS, BOOMERANG, and IDE^{al} within the tool CogniCrypt. By the use of the domain-specific language CrySL, CogniCrypt is able to statically detect cryptographic misuses.

Acknowledgments My high appreciation to all my co-authors of the work, who largely shaped and influenced this work: Karim Ali, Eric Bodden, Stefan Krüger, Johannes Lerch, Mira Mezini, and Lisa Nguyen Quang Do. Also, I also want to thank the Fraunhofer-Gesellschaft for supporting this research through a Fraunhofer Attract grant.

References

1. Steven Arzt, Siegfried Rasthofer, Christian Fritz, Eric Bodden, Alexandre Bartel, Jacques Klein, Yves Le Traon, Damien Octeau, and Patrick McDaniel. FlowDroid: Precise Context, Flow, Field, Object-Sensitive and Lifecycle-Aware Taint Analysis for Android Apps. In *PLDI*, 2014.
2. George Balatsouras, Kostas Ferles, George Kastrinis, and Yannis Smaragdakis. A Datalog Model of Must-Alias Analysis. In *International Workshop on State Of the Art in Java Program analysis, (SOAP)*, pages 7–12, 2017.

3. Ahmed Bouajjani, Javier Esparza, and Oded Maler. Reachability Analysis of Pushdown Automata: Application to Model-Checking. In *International Conference on Concurrency Theory (CONCUR)*, pages 135–150, 1997.
4. Ben-Chung Cheng and Wen-mei W. Hwu. Modular Interprocedural Pointer Analysis Using Access Paths: Design, Implementation, and Evaluation. In *PLDI*, pages 57–69, 2000.
5. Arnab De and Deepak D'Souza. Scalable Flow-Sensitive Pointer Analysis for Java with Strong Updates. In *ECOOP*, pages 665–687, 2012.
6. Alain Deutsch. Interprocedural May-Alias Analysis for Pointers: Beyond *k*-limiting. In *PLDI*, 1994.
7. Dino Distefano, Manuel Fähndrich, Francesco Logozzo, and Peter W. O'Hearn. Scaling static analyses at facebook. *Commun. ACM*, 62(8):62–70, 2019.
8. Manuel Egele, David Brumley, Yanick Fratantonio, and Christopher Kruegel. An Empirical Study of Cryptographic Misuse in Android Applications. In *International Conference on Computer and Communications Security (CCS)*, pages 73–84, 2013.
9. Javier Esparza, David Hansel, Peter Rossmanith, and Stefan Schwoon. Efficient Algorithms for Model Checking Pushdown Systems. In *International Conference on Computer Aided Verification (CAV)*, pages 232–247, 2000.
10. Yu Feng, Xinyu Wang, Isil Dillig, and Thomas Dillig. Bottom-Up Context-Sensitive Pointer Analysis for Java. In *Asian Symposium on Programming Languages and Systems (APLAS)*, pages 465–484, 2015.
11. Stephen J. Fink, Eran Yahav, Nurit Dor, G. Ramalingam, and Emmanuel Geay. Effective Typestate Verification in the Presence of Aliasing. In *International Symposium on Software Testing and Analysis (ISSTA)*, pages 133–144, 2006.
12. Stephen J. Fink, Eran Yahav, Nurit Dor, G. Ramalingam, and Emmanuel Geay. Effective Typestate Verification in the Presence of Aliasing. *ACM Transactions on Software Engineering and Methodology (TOSEM)*, 2008.
13. Manuel Geffken, Hannes Saffrich, and Peter Thiemann. Precise Interprocedural Side-Effect Analysis. In *International Colloquium on Theoretical Aspects of Computing (ICTAC)*, pages 188–205, 2014.
14. David Hauzar, Jan Kofron, and Pavel Bastecký. Data-Flow Analysis of Programs with Associative Arrays. In *International Workshop on Engineering Safety and Security Systems (ESSS)*, pages 56–70, 2014.
15. Brittany Johnson, Yoonki Song, Emerson R. Murphy-Hill, and Robert W. Bowdidge. Why don't Software Developers use Static Analysis Tools to Find Bugs? In *ICSE*, 2013.
16. Vineet Kahlon, Nishant Sinha, Erik Kruus, and Yun Zhang. Static Data Race Detection for Concurrent Programs with Asynchronous Calls. In *International Symposium on Foundations of Software Engineering (FSE)*, pages 13–22, 2009.
17. Uday P. Khedker, Amitabha Sanyal, and Amey Karkare. Heap Reference Analysis Using Access Graphs. *ACM Transactions on Programming Languages and Systems (TOPLAS)*, 2007.
18. Shuhei Kimura, Keisuke Hotta, Yoshiki Higo, Hiroshi Igaki, and Shinji Kusumoto. Does return null matter? In *Conference on Software Maintenance, Reengineering, and Reverse Engineering (CSMR-WCRE)*, pages 244–253, 2014.
19. P. S. Kochhar, D. Wijedasa, and D. Lo. A large scale study of multiple programming languages and code quality. In *International Conference on Software Analysis, Evolution, and Reengineering (SANER)*, 2016.
20. Stefan Krüger, Johannes Späth, Karim Ali, Eric Bodden, and Mira Mezini. CrySL: An Extensible Approach to Validating the Correct Usage of Cryptographic APIs. In *ECOOP*, 2018.
21. Akash Lal and Thomas W. Reps. Improving Pushdown System Model Checking. In *International Conference on Computer Aided Verification (CAV)*, pages 343–357, 2006.
22. Akash Lal and Thomas W. Reps. Solving Multiple Dataflow Queries Using WPDSs. In *International Symposium on Static Analysis (SAS)*, pages 93–109, 2008.

23. Akash Lal, Thomas W. Reps, and Gogul Balakrishnan. Extended Weighted Pushdown Systems. In *International Conference on Computer Aided Verification (CAV)*, pages 434–448, 2005.
24. Ondrej Lhoták and Laurie J. Hendren. Context-Sensitive Points-to Analysis: Is it Worth it? In *International Conference on Compiler Construction (CC)*, pages 47–64, 2006.
25. Yue Li, Tian Tan, Anders Møler, and Yannis Smaragdakis. Scalability-First Pointer Analysis with Self-Tuning Context-Sensitivity. In *International Symposium on Foundations of Software Engineering (FSE)*, November 2018.
26. Zhenmin Li, Lin Tan, Xuanhui Wang, Shan Lu, Yuanyuan Zhou, and Chengxiang Zhai. Have things changed now?: an empirical study of bug characteristics in modern open source software. In *Workshop on Architectural and System Support for Improving Software Dependability (ASID)*, pages 25–33, 2006.
27. V. Benjamin Livshits and Monica S. Lam. Finding Security Vulnerabilities in Java Applications with Static Analysis. In *USENIX Security Symposium*, 2005.
28. Ravi Mangal, Mayur Naik, and Hongseok Yang. A Correspondence Between Two Approaches to Interprocedural Analysis in the Presence of Join. In *European Symposium on Programming (ESOP)*, pages 513–533, 2014.
29. Michael C. Martin, V. Benjamin Livshits, and Monica S. Lam. Finding Application Errors and Security Flaws Using PQL: A Program Query Language. In *OOPSLA*, pages 365–383, 2005.
30. Sarah Nadi, Stefan Krüger, Mira Mezini, and Eric Bodden. Jumping Through Hoops: Why do Java Developers Struggle with Cryptography APIs? In *ICSE*, pages 935–946, 2016.
31. Mangala Gowri Nanda and Saurabh Sinha. Accurate Interprocedural Null-Dereference Analysis for Java. In *ICSE*, pages 133–143, 2009.
32. Thomas W. Reps. Undecidability of Context-Sensitive Data-Independence Analysis. *ACM Transactions on Programming Languages and Systems*, pages 162–186, 2000.
33. Thomas W. Reps, Susan Horwitz, and Shmuel Sagiv. Precise Interprocedural Dataflow Analysis via Graph Reachability. In *POPL*, pages 49–61, 1995.
34. Thomas W. Reps, Stefan Schwoon, Somesh Jha, and David Melski. Weighted Pushdown Systems and their Application to Interprocedural Dataflow Analysis. *Science of Computer Programming*, pages 206–263, 2005.
35. H. G. Rice. Classes of Recursively Enumerable Sets and Their Decision Problems. *Transactions of the American Mathematical Society*, 1953.
36. Caitlin Sadowski, Edward Aftandilian, Alex Eagle, Liam Miller-Cushon, and Ciera Jaspan. Lessons from building static analysis tools at google. *Communications of the ACM (CACM)*, pages 58–66, 2018.
37. Johannes Späth. *Synchronized Pushdown Systems for Pointer and Data-Flow Analysis*. PhD thesis, University of Paderborn, Germany, 2019.
38. Johannes Späth, Karim Ali, and Eric Bodden. IDE^{al}: Efficient and Precise Alias-Aware Dataflow Analysis. In *OOPSLA*, 2017.
39. Johannes Späth, Karim Ali, and Eric Bodden. Context-, Flow- and Field-Sensitive Data-Flow Analysis using Synchronized Pushdown Systems. In *POPL*, 2019.
40. Johannes Späth, Lisa Nguyen Quang Do, Karim Ali, and Eric Bodden. Boomerang: Demand-Driven Flow- and Context-Sensitive Pointer Analysis for Java. In *ECOOP*, 2016.
41. Omer Tripp, Marco Pistoia, Patrick Cousot, Radhia Cousot, and Salvatore Guarnieri. Andromeda: Accurate and Scalable Security Analysis of Web Applications. In *International Conference on Fundamental Approaches to Software Engineering (FASE)*, pages 210–225, 2013.
42. Omer Tripp, Marco Pistoia, Stephen J. Fink, Manu Sridharan, and Omri Weisman. TAJ: Effective Taint Analysis of Web Applications. In *PLDI*, pages 87–97, 2009.
43. Dacong Yan, Guoqing (Harry) Xu, and Atanas Rountev. Demand-Driven Context-Sensitive Alias Analysis for Java. In *International Symposium on Software Testing and Analysis (ISSTA)*, pages 155–165, 2011.

Software Developers' Work Habits and Expertise: Empirical Studies on Sketching, Code Plagiarism, and Expertise Development

Sebastian Baltes

Abstract Analyzing and understanding software developers' work habits and resulting needs is an essential prerequisite to improve software development practice. In our research, we utilize different qualitative and quantitative research methods to empirically investigate three underexplored aspects of software development: First, we analyze how software developers use sketches and diagrams in their daily work and derive requirements for better tool support. Then, we explore to what degree developers copy code from the popular online platform Stack Overflow without adhering to license requirements and motivate why this behavior may lead to legal issues for affected open source software projects. Finally, we describe a novel theory of software development expertise and identify factors fostering or hindering the formation of such expertise. Besides, we report on methodological implications of our research and present the open dataset SOTorrent, which supports researchers in analyzing the origin, evolution, and usage of content on Stack Overflow. The common goal for all studies we conducted was to better understand software developers' work practices. Our findings support researchers and practitioners in making data-informed decisions when developing new tools or improving processes related to either the specific work habits we studied or expertise development in general.

1 Introduction

A work habit, which is a "settled tendency or usual manner of behavior," can positively or negatively influence software developers' daily work. Knowing and understanding such work habits and resulting needs is an essential prerequisite to improve the existing software development processes and tools. However, the software engineering research community is often criticized for not addressing the

S. Baltes (✉)
The University of Adelaide, Adelaide, SA, Australia
e-mail: sebastian.baltes@adelaide.edu.au

© The Author(s) 2020   47
M. Felderer et al. (eds.), *Ernst Denert Award for Software Engineering 2019*,
https://doi.org/10.1007/978-3-030-58617-1_4

problems that practitioners actually face during their work [1]. At the same time, software developers' beliefs are rather based on their personal experience than on empirical findings [2]. To fill this gap between academia and practice, we conducted several empirical studies investigating different aspects of *software developers' work habits and expertise*.

While the goal guiding all empirical studies we conducted was to gain a better understanding of software developers' work practices, we drew different conclusions for each of the studied phenomena: Based on our results, we developed novel tool prototypes to better support software developers' sketching and diagramming workflows, we reached out to developers to make them aware of possible licensing issues in their software projects due to code copied from Stack Overflow, and we provide recommendations for researchers, developers, and employers how to utilize our findings on software development expertise and its formation.

For the first part of this research project (see Sect. 2), we studied how software developers use *sketches and diagrams* in their daily work. At the time we started our research, an overall picture of developers' work habits related to the creation and usage of sketches and diagrams was missing. To fill this gap, we conducted an exploratory field study in different software companies, an online survey with software practitioners, and an observational study with software developers. We found that developers frequently create and use sketches and diagrams and that they consider many of those visual artifacts to be helpful in understanding related source code. However, we also identified a lack of tool support to archive and retrieve sketches and diagrams documenting different aspects of software systems. Thus, based on our findings, we derived requirements to better support developers' sketching and diagramming workflows and implemented those requirements in two tool prototypes, named *SketchLink* and *LivelySketches*, which we then evaluated in formative user studies.

The second part (see Sect. 3) presents an extensive empirical study on a rather negative work habit: We investigated to what degree developers adhere to Stack Overflow's license requirements when copying code snippets published on that platform—or, in other words, to what extent they commit *code plagiarism*. Since many developers use the online question-and-answer platform Stack Overflow on a daily basis [3], it is an essential part of their daily work life. If developers copy code snippets from that platform into their open source software projects without adhering to the corresponding license requirements, legal issues may arise. After describing the legal situation around Stack Overflow code snippets, we give a first estimate of how frequently developers copy such snippets into public GitHub projects without the required attribution, provide an analysis of licensing conflicts, and present results from an online survey, which suggest that many developers are not aware of the licensing situation and its implications. Besides publishing our empirical results, we reached out to owners of open source GitHub projects to make them aware of possible licensing conflicts in their projects.

In the third part of this research project (see Sect. 4), we present a first conceptual theory of *software development expertise* that is grounded in the related literature and three online surveys with software developers. The connection to work habits is that, by learning from past experience, developers may adapt their work habits over time. Moreover, the existing habits related to self-improvement and learning may shape the path of an individual from being a novice toward being an expert in software development. Previously, the software engineering research community was lacking a comprehensive theory on what constitutes software development expertise and how such expertise is formed. Our theory describes important properties of software development expertise and factors fostering or hindering its formation, including how developers' performance may decline over time. Based on that theory, we provide recommendations for researchers who want to study expertise formation, developers who want to improve their software development skills, and employers who want to build a work environment supporting expertise development of their staff.

While the first three sections describe the main contributions of this research project, in Sect. 5, we reflect on *methodological and ethical issues* we faced when sampling software developers for the online surveys we conducted. The goal of that chapter is to inform the research community which strategies worked best for us, but we also want to start a discussion about the ethics of different sampling strategies that researchers currently use. To conclude this article, and to corroborate our *open data* efforts, we present the open dataset *SOTorrent*, which we created in the context of our research on Stack Overflow code snippets, described in Sect. 3. Besides explaining how we built the dataset, we use it to conduct a first analysis of the evolution of content on Stack Overflow and to investigate code snippets copied from external sources into Stack Overflow and duplicates of code snippets within Stack Overflow. We continue to maintain the dataset to support further research on the origin, evolution, and usage of content on Stack Overflow.

2   Sketching: Developers' Usage of Sketches and Diagrams in Practice

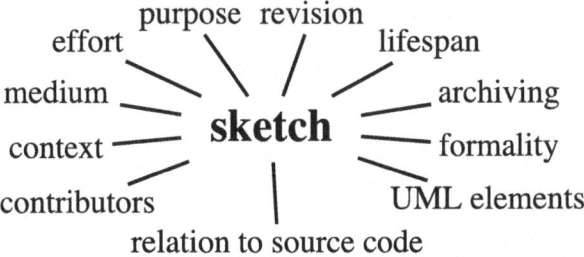

Fig. 1 The 11 dimensions of a sketch or diagram in software development that we used to structure and guide our research

Communication is omnipresent in software development. Requirements are communicated from prospective users to the developers implementing the software, the general architecture is communicated within the development team, developers communicate with each other during pair programming, and after deployment, issues are reported back to developers. Such information flows involve diverse channels [4], including face-to-face communication [5, 6], email [7], videoconferencing [5, 6], and team collaboration tools [8]. Especially in collocated settings, developers use informal sketches and diagrams for communication [9]. Those visual artifacts, spanning different types of media [10], support developers in designing new and understanding existing software systems [11]. Nevertheless, when we started our research on sketches and diagrams in software development practice, an overall picture of how developers use those visual artifacts was missing. Therefore, in the corresponding chapter of the dissertation, we first motivate our notion of sketch *dimensions* to capture the most important characteristics of visual artifacts used in software development (see Fig. 1) and then present the design and results of a mixed-methods study we conducted to investigate how software practitioners use such artifacts. Our research included an exploratory field study in three different software companies, an online survey with 394 participants, and an observational study with six pair programming teams. After describing the state of practice and resulting needs of software practitioners working with sketches and diagrams, we present two tool prototypes that we developed in response to the results of our empirical investigation. The content of this chapter is based on four peer-reviewed publications [10, 12, 13, 14].

Contributions

- A **characterization** of sketches and diagrams in software development practice, which is grounded in related work and in a field study we conducted in three different software companies.
- An assessment of 11 different dimensions of sketches and diagrams in software development using an **online survey** with 394 software practitioners.
- An analysis how developers communicate in a **pair-programming** setting when **locating performance bugs**, including an investigation of the **role of sketches** in this scenario.
- A presentation of two **tool prototypes** supporting software developers' sketching and diagramming workflows.

Overall, we found that software practitioners frequently create and use such visual artifacts. Our online survey revealed that sketches and diagrams are often informal but are considered to be a valuable resource, documenting many aspects of the software development workflow. We showed how sketches are related to source code artifacts on different levels of abstraction and that roughly half of them were rated as helpful to understand the source code. As documentation is frequently poorly written and out of date, sketches could fill in this gap and serve as a supplement to conventional documentation such as source code comments or other textual resources. The majority of sketches and diagrams were created on analog media such as paper or whiteboard. Many of them were archived, but our survey participants also named technical issues, for example, that there is no good technique to keep (digital versions of) sketches together with source code. In response to this observation, we developed the tool prototype *SketchLink*, which assists developers in archiving and retrieving sketches related to certain source code artifacts. Regarding the evolution of sketches, our qualitative results indicated that it is a common use case for sketches to be initially created on analog media like paper or whiteboards and then, potentially after some revisions, they end up as an archived digital sketch. To support such workflows, we developed a second tool prototype named *LivelySketches*, which supports transitions from analog to digital media and back. One direction for future work is to merge the features of both prototypes and evaluate the resulting tool in larger context. Moreover, with techniques such as *graphic facilitation* and *sketchnoting* becoming more and more popular, analyzing potential use cases for those techniques in software development projects emerged as another direction for future work. We already interviewed graphic facilitators who worked in software development projects, but also software developers and architects with sketching experience. Based on those interviews, we will derive recommendations for applying visualization techniques in different phases of software development projects.

3   Code Plagiarism: Stack Overflow Code Snippets in GitHub Projects

Stack Overflow is the most popular question-and-answer website for software developers, providing a large amount of copyable code snippets. Using those snippets raises maintenance and legal issues. Stack Overflow's license (CC BY-SA) requires attribution, that is referencing the original question or answer, and requires derived work to adopt a compatible license. While there is a heated debate on Stack Overflow's license model for code snippets and the required attribution, little is known about the extent to which snippets are copied from Stack Overflow without proper attribution. To fill this gap, we conducted a large-scale empirical study analyzing software developers' usage and attribution of non-trivial Java code snippets from Stack Overflow answers in public GitHub projects. We followed three different approaches to triangulate an estimate for the ratio of unattributed usages and conducted two online surveys with software developers to complement our results. For the different sets of GitHub projects that we analyzed, the ratio of projects containing files with a reference to Stack Overflow varied between 3.3 and 11.9%. We found that at most 1.8% of all analyzed repositories containing code from Stack Overflow used the code in a way compatible with CC BY-SA. Moreover, we estimate that at most a quarter of the copied code snippets from Stack Overflow are attributed as required. Of the surveyed developers, almost one half admitted copying code from Stack Overflow without attribution and about two-thirds were not aware of the license of Stack Overflow code snippets and its implications.

The content of this chapter is based on a peer-reviewed journal publication [15]. Moreover, some results have also been published in an extended abstract before [16].

Contributions

- A thorough description of the **legal situation** around Stack Overflow code snippets.
- A **triangulated estimation** of the **attribution ratio** of Stack Overflow code snippets in public GitHub projects.
- An analysis of possible **licensing conflicts** for the GitHub projects containing code from Stack Overflow.
- A qualitative analysis of **how developers refer to** Stack Overflow content.
- An **online survey** suggesting that many **developers are not aware** of the licensing of Stack Overflow code snippets and its implications.

Our research revealed that at most one quarter of the code snippets copied from Stack Overflow into public GitHub Java projects are attributed as required by Stack Overflow's license (CC BY-SA). Moreover, we found that between 3.3 and 11.9% of the analyzed GitHub repositories contained a file with a reference to Stack Overflow (see Table 1). We identified only 1.8% of the GitHub projects with copies of Stack Overflow code snippets to attribute the copy and to use a license that is share-alike compatible with Stack Overflow's license. For the other 98.2% of the projects, especially the share-alike requirement of CC BY-SA may lead to licensing conflicts. Two online surveys have shown that many developers admit copying code from Stack Overflow without attribution. We also found that many of them are not aware of the licensing situation and its implications. In the course of our research on Stack Overflow code snippets, we built the *SOTorrent* dataset (see Sect. 6), which we continue to maintain. Beside closely following how other researchers use the dataset to study different questions related to code on Stack Overflow, we will continue to investigate how such code snippets are maintained and how their evolution can be better supported. Another direction for future work, which is not limited to Stack Overflow, is to build better tool support for developers dealing with online code snippets. On the one hand, continuous integration tools could check whether commits add non-trivial code snippets from online resources to a project; on the other hand, tools could support developers in understanding license compatibility not only for whole software libraries, but also on the level of individual code snippets copied from online resources. Those efforts can help mitigating legal threats for open source projects that intentionally or unintentionally use code from diverse sources.

Table 1 Summary of results regarding attribution of snippets copied from Stack Overflow (SO): distinct references to answers (A) or questions (Q) on SO in the Java files from GitHub analyzed in each phase of our research; number of analyzed files and repositories, files/repos containing a reference to SO, files/repos containing a copy of a SO snippet, attributed copies of SO snippets

Ph.	References		Files				Repositories		
	A	Q	Count	Ref	Copy	Attr	Count	Ref	Copy
1	5014	16,298	13.3m	18,605	4198	402	336k	11,086	3291
	23.5%	76.5%		0.09%	0.03%	9.6%		3.3%	1.0%
2	209	463	445k	634	297	70	2313	274	199
	31.1%	68.9%		0.14%	0.07%	23.6%		11.9%	8.6%
3	1551	4843	1.7m	5354	1369	104	64,281	3536	1332
	24.3%	75.7%		0.31%	0.08%	7.6%		5.5%	2.1%

4 Expertise Development: Toward a Theory of Software Development Expertise

Software development includes diverse tasks such as implementing new features, analyzing requirements, and fixing bugs. Being an expert in those tasks requires a certain set of skills, knowledge, and experience. Several studies investigated individual aspects of software development expertise, but what is missing is a comprehensive theory. In this chapter, we present a first conceptual theory of software development expertise that is grounded in data from a mixed-methods survey with 335 software developers (see gray boxes in Fig. 2) and in the literature on expertise and expert performance. Our theory currently focuses on programming but already provides valuable insights for researchers, developers, and employers. The theory describes important properties of software development expertise and which factors foster or hinder its formation, including how developers' performance may decline over time. Moreover, our quantitative results show that developers' expertise self-assessments are context-dependent and that experience is not necessarily related to expertise. The content of this chapter is based on a peer-reviewed publication [17].

Contributions
- A first **conceptual theory** of **software development expertise** grounded in a survey with 335 software developers and in the literature on expertise and expert performance.
- Quantitative results that point to the **context-dependence** of software developers' **expertise self-assessments**.
- A **theory-building approach** involving inductive and deductive steps that other (software engineering) researchers can apply or adapt (see Fig. 2).

With our research, we identified different characteristics of software development experts, but also factors fostering or hindering the formation of software development expertise. Besides building a first conceptual theory, we found that expertise self-assessments are context-dependent and do not always correspond to experience measured in years. Researchers can use our findings when designing studies involving expertise self-assessments. We recommend to explicitly describe what distinguishes novices from experts in the specific setting under study when asking participants for expertise self-assessments. Our theory enables researchers to design new experiments, but also to re-evaluate results from previous experiments. Software developers can use our results to learn which properties are distinctive for experts in their field, and which behaviors may lead to becoming a better software developer. For example, the concept of deliberate practice, and in particular having challenging goals, a supportive work environment, and getting feedback from peers are important factors. For "senior" developers, our results provide suggestions for being a good mentor. Mentors should know that they are considered to be an important source for feedback and motivation, and that being patient and being open-minded are desired characteristics. We also provide first results on the consequences of age-related performance decline, which is an important direction for future work. Employers can learn what typical reasons for demotivation among their employees are, and how they can build a work environment supporting the self-improvement of their staff. Besides obvious strategies such as offering training sessions or paying for conference visits, our results suggest that employers should think carefully about how information is shared between their developers and also between development teams and other departments of the company. Finally, employers should make sure to have a good mix of continuity and change in their software development process because non-challenging work, often caused by tasks becoming routine, is an important demotivating factor for software developers. One important direction for future work, which emerged in the course of our research, is *the role of older software developers*. Especially in industrialized countries, the demographic change leads to an older work force, since people are expected to retire later. Still, the challenges that older developers face in a competitive field like software development are largely unknown. Our study participants already mentioned different age-related challenges. We plan to study those challenges to be able to mitigate them where possible, preventing those experienced developers from dropping out of software development.

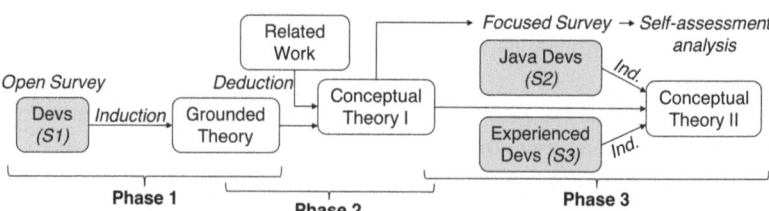

Fig. 2 Structure of our iterative theory-building approach

5   Methodological Insights: Issues in Sampling Software Developers

Online surveys like the ones we conducted for this research project are considered to be a feasible means for investigating the state of practice [18]. In particular, surveys are an important empirical method used in software engineering (SE) research that can be employed to explore and describe various characteristics of a broad population [19]. However, reaching professional software developers with surveys is a difficult task. Except for single companies or institutions that allow researchers to use a list of their employees, random sampling of software developers is impossible most of the time. Researchers therefore often rely on the available subjects, which is known as *convenience sampling*. Applying non-random sampling techniques like convenience sampling may lead to biased samples with limited external validity. To mitigate the threats to external validity, researchers need detailed knowledge about the population of software developers they want to target, but this information is often not available. Further, some of the sampling techniques that researchers employ raise ethical concerns, such as contacting developers on GitHub using email addresses users did not provide for this purpose. In this chapter, we summarize what we learned while conducting online surveys with software developers. The content of this chapter is based on a peer-reviewed publication [20].

Contributions
- **Experience reports** for different survey sampling strategies.
- Presentation of the idea of a **systematic database with software developer demographics** to assess the external validity of surveys conducted using non-random sampling techniques.
- Building awareness about **ethical issues** that may arise with sampling approaches that researchers currently utilize.

We found that the most efficient and effective sampling strategies were to use public media and "testimonials" that advertise the survey. We also highlighted the importance of gatekeepers who provide access to companies or communities. Another finding is that, to be able to assess the external validity of studies involving non-random samples, researchers need a collection of typical software developer demographics, which currently does not exist. Using a systematic literature review, one could collect published demographics about developers. Further, authors of studies with software developers could be contacted and asked to provide basic demographic information about their participants, if available. This information, together with the data from the Stack Overflow developer surveys, would be a solid basis to assess the external validity of future studies. Conferences and journals may recommend authors to describe certain key demographics for published studies, and reviewers could motivate authors to explicitly address their sampling approach and effects on the generalizability of their results. We also pointed at ethical issues with some of the sampling techniques researchers currently employ, in particular using email addresses collected from GitHub to contact developers.

6 Open Data: Building and Maintaining the SOTorrent Dataset

For all studies conducted in the context of this research project, we provide supplementary material packages that enable other researchers to reproduce our results. Besides publishing (anonymized) data on the preserved archive *Zenodo*, we also published the software and scripts used to retrieve and analyze that data. Moreover, pre- or postprints of all papers are available online. Beside these general open science efforts, in this chapter, we want to particularly highlight the open dataset *SOTorrent*[1] that we created to support future research about code snippets on Stack Overflow. The dataset allows researchers to investigate and understand the evolution of Stack Overflow content on the level of individual text and code blocks, which is not possible with the official data dump that Stack Overflow provides. Beside supporting our own research, we published and promoted the dataset to be used by other researchers. Those efforts resulted in the dataset being selected as the official mining challenge of the *16th International Conference on Mining Software Repositories (MSR 2019)* [21].

The content of this chapter is based on two peer-reviewed publications: One full paper describing the creation of *SOTorrent* and first analyses using the dataset [20] as well as our accepted mining challenge proposal [21]. Moreover, we present additional analyses that we conducted for an upcoming journal extension of our initial *SOTorrent* paper (see research questions three and four).

Contributions

- An open **dataset** that allows researchers to investigate and understand the evolution of Stack Overflow posts and their relation to other platforms such as GitHub.
- A thorough **evaluation of 134 string similarity metrics** regarding their applicability for reconstructing the version history of Stack Overflow text and code blocks.
- A **first analysis of the evolution** of content on Stack Overflow, including the description of a close relationship between post edits and comments.
- An **analysis of code clones** on Stack Overflow together with an investigation of possible licensing risks.

The *SOTorrent* dataset has allowed us to study the phenomenon of post editing on SO in detail. We found that a total of 13.9 million SO posts (36.1% of all posts) have been edited at least once. Many of these edits (44.1%) modify only a single line of text or code, and while posts grow over time in terms of the number of text and code blocks they contain, the size of these individual blocks is relatively stable. Interestingly, only in 6.1% of all cases are code blocks changed without corresponding changes in text blocks of the same post, suggesting that SO users

---

[1]http://sotorrent.org.

typically update the textual description accompanying code snippets when they are edited. We also found that edits are mostly made shortly after the creation of a post (78.2% of all edits are made on the same day when the post was created), and the vast majority of edits are made by post authors (87.4%)—although the remaining 12.6% will be of particular interest for our future work. The number of comments on posts without edits is significantly smaller than the number of comments on posts with edits, suggesting an interplay of these two features. We find evidence which suggests that commenting on a post on SO helps to bring attention to it. Of the comments that were made on the same day as an edit, 47.9% were made before an edit and 52.1% afterwards, typically (median value) only 18 min before or after the edit. Motivated by this quantitative analysis of the temporal relationship between edits and comments, we conducted a qualitative study and developed a visual analysis tool to explore the communication structure of SO threads. Our analysis using this tool revealed several communication and edit patterns that provide further evidence for the connection between post edits and comments. We found comments which explain, trigger, and announce edits as well as content overlap between edits and comments. The fact that SO users rely on the commenting feature to make others aware of post edits—and in some cases even duplicate content between comments and posts—suggests that users are worried that content evolution will be missed if it is buried in a comment or has been added to a post later via an edit. At the same time, we found evidence that edits can play a vital role in attracting answers to a question. In our future work, we will explore how changes to Stack Overflow's user interface could make the evolution of content more explicit and remove the need for users to repurpose the commenting feature as an awareness mechanism. Besides, we investigated code clones on SO, revealing that, just like in regular software projects, code clones on SO can affect the maintainability of posts and lead to licensing issues. Depending on the outcome of the discussion we started on Stack Overflow Meta, we plan to implement means to add the missing attribution to posts and mark threads as related based on the similarity of the code blocks they contain.

7 Summary and Future Work

In this research project, we utilized diverse research designs to empirically investigate yet underexplored aspects of *software developers' work habits and expertise.* We started by analyzing how developers use *sketches and diagrams* in their daily work, then derived requirements for tool support, and finally implemented and evaluated two tool prototypes. In a second research project, we investigated how common it is for developers to *copy non-trivial code snippets* from the popular question-and-answer platform Stack Overflow into open source software projects hosted on GitHub, without adhering to the terms of Stack Overflow's license. In that project, we also assessed developers' awareness of the licensing situation and its implications. While those first two research projects can be regarded as analyses of a rather positive and a rather negative work habit, the third project aimed at analyzing behaviors that may lead to developers becoming experts in certain software development tasks. However, we not only identified factors influencing expertise formation over time but also developed a first conceptual theory structuring the broad concept of *software development expertise*.

In the complete version of the dissertation that this article is based on, we not only present the designs and results of the different empirical studies we conducted, but also highlighted how we use those results to guide further actions. We already used our empirical results to: (1) motivate and implement novel tools to support software developers' sketching workflows, (2) inform developers about possible licensing issues in their open source software projects, (3) build a first conceptual theory of software development expertise that researchers as well as practitioners can use, (4) point to the underexplored phenomenon of age-related performance decline, (5) grow awareness in the research community about ethical implications of certain sampling strategies, motivated by participants' feedback, and (6) create an open dataset that the research community can use for future research projects on Stack Overflow content. Our work supports researchers and practitioners in making data-informed decisions when developing new tools or improving processes related to either the specific work habits we studied or expertise development in general.

References

1. Lionel Briand. Embracing the Engineering Side of Software Engineering. *IEEE Software*, July/August:92–95, 2012.
2. Prem Devanbu, Thomas Zimmermann, and Christian Bird. Belief & Evidence in Empirical Software Engineering. In Laura Dillon, Willem Visser, and Laurie Williams, editors, *38th International Conference on Software Engineering (ICSE 2016)*, pages 108–119, Austin, TX, USA, 2016. ACM.
3. Stack Exchange Inc. Stack Overflow Developer Survey Results 2018. https://insights.stackoverflow.com/survey/2018, 2018.
4. Margaret-Anne Storey, Leif Singer, Fernando Figueira Filho, Alexey Zagalsky, and Daniel M. German. How Social and Communication Channels Shape and Challenge a Participatory Culture in Software Development. *IEEE Transactions on Software Engineering*, 43(2):185–204, 2017.
5. Hayward P. Andres. A comparison of face-to-face and virtual software development teams. *Team Performance Management: An International Journal*, 8(1/2):39–48, 2002.
6. Daniela Damian, Armin Eberlein, Mildred L.G. Shaw, and Brian R. Gaines. Using Different Communication Media in Requirements Negotiation. *IEEE Software*, May/June:28–36, 2000.
7. Christian Bird, Alex Gourley, Prem Devanbu, Michael Gertz, and Anand Swaminathan. Mining Email Social Networks. In Stephan Diehl, Harald C. Gall, and Ahmed E. Hassan, editors, *3rd International Workshop on Mining Software Repositories (MSR 2006)*, pages 137–143, Shanghai, China, 2006. ACM.
8. Bin Lin, Alexey Zagalsky, Margaret-Anne Storey, and Alexander Serebrenik. Why Developers are Slacking Off: Understanding How Software Teams Use Slack. In Darren Gergle and Meredith Ringel Morris, editors, *19th ACM Conference on Computer Supported Cooperative Work and Social Computing (CSCW 2016): Companion*, pages 333–336, New York, NY, USA, 2016. ACM.

9. Uri Dekel and James D. Herbsleb. Notation and representation in collaborative object-oriented design: An observational study. In Richard P. Gabriel, David F. Bacon, Cristina Videira Lopes, and Guy L. Steele Jr., editors, *22nd ACM SIGPLAN Conference on Object-Oriented Programming, Systems, Languages, and Applications (OOPSLA 2007)*, pages 261–280, Montreal, QC, Canada, 2007. ACM.

10. Sebastian Baltes and Stephan Diehl. Sketches and diagrams in practice. In Shing-Chi Cheung, Alessandro Orso, and Margaret-Anne D. Storey, editors, *22nd ACM SIGSOFT International Symposium on Foundations of Software Engineering (FSE 2014)*, pages 530–541, Hong Kong, China, 2014. ACM.

11. Mauro Cherubini, Gina Venolia, Robert DeLine, and Andrew J. Ko. Let's go to the whiteboard: How and why software developers use drawings. In Mary Beth Rosson and David J. Gilmore, editors, *2007 Conference on Human Factors in Computing Systems (CHI 2007)*, pages 557–566, San Jose, CA, USA, 2007. ACM.

12. Sebastian Baltes, Peter Schmitz, and Stephan Diehl. Linking sketches and diagrams to source code artifacts. In Shing-Chi Cheung, Alessandro Orso, and Margaret-Anne D. Storey, editors, *22nd ACM SIGSOFT International Symposium on Foundations of Software Engineering (FSE 2014)*, pages 743–746, Hong Kong, China, 2014. ACM.

13. Sebastian Baltes, Fabrice Hollerich, and Stephan Diehl. Round-Trip Sketches: Supporting the Lifecycle of Software Development Sketches from Analog to Digital and Back. In Kang Zhang, Ivan Beschastnikh, and Andrea Mocci, editors, *2017 IEEE Working Conference on Software Visualization (VISSOFT 2017)*, pages 94–98, Shanghai, China, 2017. IEEE.

14. Sebastian Baltes, Oliver Moseler, Fabian Beck, and Stephan Diehl. Navigate, Understand, Communicate: How Developers Locate Performance Bugs. In Qing Wang, Guenther Ruhe, Jeff Carver, and Oscar Dieste, editors, *9th International Symposium on Empirical Software Engineering and Measurement (ESEM 2015)*, pages 225–234, Beijing, China, 2015. IEEE.

15. Sebastian Baltes and Stephan Diehl. Usage and Attribution of Stack Overflow Code Snippets in GitHub Projects. *Empirical Software Engineering*, Online First:1–37, 2018.

16. Sebastian Baltes, Richard Kiefer, and Stephan Diehl. Attribution required: Stack overflow code snippets in GitHub projects. In Sebastián Uchitel, Alessandro Orso, and Martin P. Robillard, editors, *39th International Conference on Software Engineering (ICSE 2017), Companion Volume*, pages 161–163, Buenos Aires, Argentina, 2017. IEEE Computer Society.

17. Sebastian Baltes and Stephan Diehl. Towards a Theory of Software Development Expertise. In Gary Leavens, Alessandro Garcia, and Corina Pasareanu, editors, *26th ACM Joint European Software Engineering Conference and Symposium on the Foundations of Software Engineering (ESEC/FSE 2018)*, pages 187–200, Lake Buena Vista, FL, USA, 2018. ACM.

18. Aileen Cater-Steel, Mark Toleman, and Terry Rout. Addressing the Challenges of Replications of Surveys in Software Engineering Research. In Ross Jeffery, June Verner, and Guilherme H. Travassos, editors, *2005 International Symposium on Empirical Software Engineering (ISESE 2005)*, pages 10–pp, Noosa Heads, Queensland, Australia, 2005. IEEE.

19. Steve Easterbrook, Janice Singer, Margaret-Anne Storey, and Daniela Damian. Chapter 11: Selecting Empirical Methods for Software Engineering Research. In Forrest Shull, Janice Singer, and Dag I.K. Sjoberg, editors, *Guide to Advanced Empirical Software Engineering*, pages 285–311. Springer, London, UK, 2008.

20. Sebastian Baltes and Stephan Diehl. Worse Than Spam: Issues In Sampling Software Developers. In Marcela Genero, Andreas Jedlitschka, and Magne Jorgensen, editors, *10th International Symposium on Empirical Software Engineering and Measurement (ESEM 2016)*, pages 52:1–52:6, Ciudad Real, Spain, 2016. ACM.

21. Sebastian Baltes, Christoph Treude, and Stephan Diehl. SOTorrent: Studying the Origin, Evolution, and Usage of Stack Overflow Code Snippets. In Margaret-Anne Storey, Bram Adams, and Sonia Haiduc, editors, *16th International Conference on Mining Software Repositories (MSR 2019)*, Montreal, QC, Canada, 2019. IEEE.

Applied Artifact-Based Analysis for Architecture Consistency Checking

Timo Greifenberg, Steffen Hillemacher, and Katrin Hölldobler

Abstract The usage of models within model-driven software development aims at facilitating complexity management of the system under development and closing the gap between the problem and the solution domain. Utilizing model-driven software development (MDD) tools for agile development can also increase the complexity within a project. The huge number of different artifacts and relations, their different kinds, and the high degree of automation hinder the understanding, maintenance, and evolution within MDD projects. A systematic approach to understand and manage MDD projects with a focus on its artifacts and corresponding relations is necessary to handle the complexity. The artifact-based analysis presented in this paper is such an approach. This paper gives an overview of different contributions of the artifact-based analysis but focuses on a specific kind of analysis: architecture consistency checking of model-driven development projects. By applying this kind of analyses, differences between the desired architecture and the actual architecture of the project at a specific point in time can be revealed.

1 Introduction

The complexity of developing modern software systems or software-intensive systems continues to rise. Software is already considered the most important factor of the competition within the automotive industry, which leads to an increasing complexity especially in automotive software [EF17]. Further examples of complex systems with a high amount of software are cloud-based systems [KRR14], cyberphysical systems (CPS) [Lee08], or Internet of Things (IoT) [AIM10]. When developing complex software systems, there is a wide conceptual gap between the problem and the implementation domains [FR07]. Bridging this gap by extensive handcrafting of implementations can lead to accidental complexities that make

T. Greifenberg (✉) · S. Hillemacher · K. Hölldobler
Software Engineering, RWTH Aachen University, Aachen, Germany
e-mail: greifenberg@se-rwth.de; hillemacher@se-rwth.de; hoelldobler@se-rwth.de

© The Author(s) 2020
M. Felderer et al. (eds.), *Ernst Denert Award for Software Engineering 2019*,
https://doi.org/10.1007/978-3-030-58617-1_5

the development of complex software difficult and costly [FR07]. Additionally, some development processes demand tracing of development artifacts [MHDZ16]. Creating and maintaining such relationships consequently lead to additional effort during the development.

In order to be able to control the complexity of the software as well as to close the conceptual gap between problem and solution domain, approaches of the field of model-driven software development (MDD) arose. MDD technologies have been successfully applied in industrial software development processes, which lead to improved quality and productivity [WHR14]. Platform-independent models [OMG14] provide a means to abstract from technical aspects of the solution domain, making the complexity easier to control. Such models of the problem domain can often be developed directly by domain experts. The usage of domain-specific languages (DSL) for modeling different aspects of the system helps to focus on single aspects of the system in more detail [CCF+15]. The resulting domain-specific models can then be used as primary input for an MDD tool chain. These tool chains can guarantee the conformity of models (both, of single models and between several models), analyze their contents, and automatically create parts of the software product to be developed. Such an automated MDD build process removes the necessity of manual synchronization between models and source code. After adapting the models, the corresponding source code can be automatically recreated without any additional effort. Hence, the use of MDD approaches aims for a more efficient and effective software development process [BCW12], ultimately, reducing manual effort, improving software quality through systematic translation of domain-specific models into the source code, and lowering the development costs.

In MDD projects, not only a large number of different artifacts caused by the complexity of the software exist, but also a multitude of different artifact types. Examples are models, templates, and grammar files, which are required by special technologies to create MDD tools. Between these specific types of artifacts, heterogeneous and complex relationships exist, thus understanding them is vital for MDD tool developers. Examples for such relationships are imports between model artifacts, artifacts that are used as input to automatically generate a set of target artifacts, or artifacts containing each other.

The high amount and complexity of these dependencies create a number of new challenges for MDD projects [GHR17]: (1) poor maintainability in case of necessary changes due to unnecessary or unforeseen artifact relationships, (2) inefficient build processes that perform unnecessary process steps or cannot be executed incrementally, (3) long development times because poorly organized artifact dependencies cause errors, and (4) prevention of reuse of individual tool components or parts of the generated product caused by unnecessary artifact relations. Due to the large number of different artifacts and relationships, the multitude of artifact and relationship types, the use of special MDD tools and the high degree of automation, a systematic approach is necessary to handle the complexity in MDD projects. For the existing projects where no such approach was used, reverse engineering techniques can help to reconstruct how artifacts are structured. Furthermore, relations between artifacts can be reconstructed, which makes it easier to understand the dependencies as well as provide a way to analyze the potential of process optimization. Such analyses of artifacts and their relations are presented as artifact-based analyses [Gre19].

This paper gives an overview on the artifact-based analysis [Gre19] and, thus, presents content that is already published. It cannot cover all the contributions in all detail, which leads to presenting some of the topics in a simplified way or omitting some details in discussions. Moreover, this work focusses just on a single kind of artifact-based analysis: architecture consistency checking of MDD projects. Compared to the original thesis [Gre19], an additional case of application succeeding the former work is described in this paper in Sect. 4.2.

The main contribution of the original thesis are the methods and concepts for the artifact-based analysis of model-driven software development projects [Gre19]. The contribution consists of:

- A modeling technique for modeling artifact relationships and for the specification of associated analyses.
- A concrete model, which describes artifact relationships in MontiCore-based development projects.
- A methodology for using the modeling technique.
- A tool chain that supports artifact-based analyses.

2 Foundations

In this section, the modeling languages and model-processing tools used in this approach are presented. Using these to describe artifacts and artifact relationships is explained in Sect. 3.

2.1 UML/P

The UML/P language family [Rum16, Rum17] is a language profile of the Unified Modeling Language (UML) [OMG15], which is a modeling standard developed by the OMG [OMG17]. Due to the large number of languages, their fields of application, and the lack of formalization, the UML is not directly suitable for model-driven software development. However, this could be achieved by restricting the modeling languages and language constructs allowed as done in the UML/P language family. A textual version of the UML/P, which can be used in MDD projects, was developed [Sch12]. The approach for the artifact-based analysis of MDD projects uses the languages Class Diagram (CD), Object Diagram (OD), and the Object Constraint Language (OCL).

2.1.1 Class Diagrams

Class diagrams serve to represent the structure of software systems. They form the central element for modeling software systems with the UML and are therefore the most important notation. Using class diagrams primarily, classes and their relationships are modeled. In addition, enums and interfaces, associated properties such as attributes, modifiers, and method signatures as well as various types of relationships and their cardinalities can be modeled.

In addition to being used to represent the technical, structural view of a software system, i.e., as the description of source code structures, class diagrams can be used in analysis to structure concepts in the real world [Rum16]. Especially for this use case, an even more restrictive variant of the UML/P Class Diagrams was developed: the language Class Diagram for Analysis (CD4A) [Rot17]. As a part of this approach, CD4A is used to model structures in model-based development projects.

2.1.2 Object Diagrams

Object diagrams are suitable for the specification of exemplary data of a software system. They describe a state of the system at a concrete point in time. ODs can conform to the structure of an associated class diagram. A check, whether an object diagram corresponds to the predefined structure of a class diagram is in general not trivial. For this reason, an approach for an Alloy [Jac11]-based verification technique was developed [MRR11].

In object diagrams, objects and the links between objects are modeled. The modeling of the object state is done by specifying attributes and assigned values. Depending on the intended use, object diagrams can describe a required, represent prohibited or existing situation of the software system. In addition to the concepts described in the original thesis [Sch12], the current version of the UML/P OD language allows the definition of hierarchically nested objects. This has the advantage that hierarchical relationships can also be displayed as such in the object diagrams. Listing 1 shows an example of a hierarchical OD with two nested objects. In this work, CDs are not used to describe the classes of an implementation, but used for descriptions on a conceptual level, objects of associated object diagrams also represent concepts of the problem domain instead of objects of a software system. In this approach, object diagrams are used to describe analysis data, i.e., they reflect the current state of the project at the conceptual level.

```
 1  objectdiagram Students {                                    OD
 2
 3    Max:Person {
 4      id = 1;
 5      firstName = "Max";
 6      name = "Mustermann";
 7      address = address1:Address {
 8        street = "Ahornstraße";
 9        city = "Aachen";
10        houseNumber = 55;
11        country = "Germany";
12      };
13    };
14  }
```

Listing 1 Example OD with two hierarchically nested objects

2.1.3 Object Constraint Language

The OCL is a specification language of the UML, which allows to model additional conditions of other UML languages. For example, the OCL can be used to specify invariants of class diagrams, conditions in sequence diagrams and to specify pre- or post-conditions of methods. The OCL variant of UML/P (OCL/P) is a Java-based variant of OCL. This approach uses the OCL/P variant only. OCL is only used in conjunction with class diagrams throughout this approach. OCL expressions are modeled within class diagram artifacts.

2.2 MontiCore

MontiCore [GKR+06, KRV08, GKR+08, KRV10, Kra10, Völl1, HR17] is a Language Workbench for the efficient development of compositional modeling languages. Figure 1 gives an overview of the structure and workflow of MontiCore-based generators.

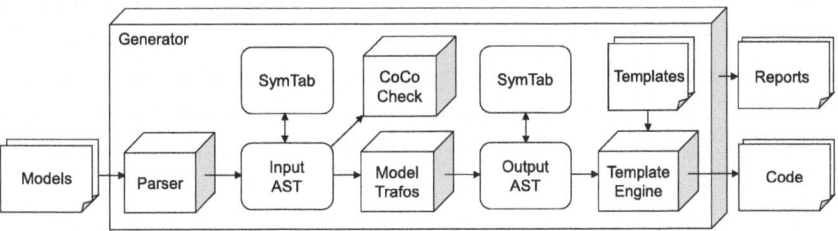

Fig. 1 Structure and execution of MontiCore-based generators

MontiCore languages are primarily specified using context-free grammars. MontiCore uses a grammar file as input to generate a parser, a data structure for abstract syntax trees (AST), and an implementation of the visitor design pattern [GHJV95] for the AST data structure. The AST data structure can be extended by a symbol table data structure that can be partially generated. Symbol tables act as a model interface and offer a way to dynamically load other model artifacts. Thus, symbol tables provide an integrated processing of multiple models of different modeling languages. By creating well-formedness rules, the so-called context conditions (CoCo), additional conditions can be added to the rules given by the grammar. These conditions are checked on the coherent data structure consisting of AST and symbol table.

Prior to the generation, model-to-model (M2M) transformation can be used to prepare AST and symbol table. These can either be implemented in the form of Java code or defined using special transformation languages [Wei12, Höl18]. A methodology for creating new transformation languages is also available [HRW15].

Next, the source code of the system in development can be generated by template-based code generation. As a by-product, additional reports are generated, which include relevant events of the last generation run or summarize the generation process.

MontiCore, thus, generates an infrastructure for processing models, checking them according to their well-formedness rules, transforming them using M2M transformations, as well as for generating source code artifacts. Moreover, MontiCore offers a runtime environment (RTE) providing functions and data structures which can be used by both the generated and handwritten parts of MontiCore-based tools. MontiCore has already been used to create languages and related tools in various domains including Automotive [RSW+15], robotics [AHRW17], and cloud applications [NPR13].

2.3   Architecture Consistency Checking

Architectural reconstruction and architectural consistency checking (ACC) are techniques that are used in the area of software architecture. Their goal is to compare the current state of a software architecture (the actual architecture or descriptive architecture) with the planned architecture (also called target architecture or prescriptive architecture). The following definitions of basic terms are taken from [TMD09]. The term architecture degradation is defined as

The resulting discrepancy between a system's prescriptive and descriptive architecture.

Further, the architectural drift is defined as

> The introduction of principal design decisions into a system's descriptive architecture that (a) are not included in, encompassed by, or implied by the prescriptive architecture, but which do not violate any of the prescriptive architecture's design decisions.

Another term is the architectural erosion defined as

> The introduction of architectural design decisions into a system's descriptive architecture that violate its prescriptive architecture.

In this work, the result of the calculation of architectural degradation is called difference architecture. Such a difference architecture, thus, contains all differences between the target and the actual architecture. Furthermore, it combines the parts of the architectural drift with those of architectural erosion. Both, the absence of expected relationships considered as architectural drift and unindended relationships considered as architectural erosion, are examined as part of this work.

In order to retrieve the difference architecture, the actual architecture must be compared to the target architecture. For this comparison, the target architecture must be specified manually, while the actual architecture is reconstructed (semi-) automatically from the source code. This process is called architectural reconstruction.

The process of architectural reconstruction distinguishes between top-down and bottom-up approaches. Bottom-up approaches are also referred to as architecture recovery [DP09]. They work fully automatically and can therefore be used even if no target architecture is available. However, they suffer from a lack of accuracy [GIM13]. By combining two different bottom-up approaches, the quality of the actual architecture during architecture recovery could be increased, which also increased the quality of the reconstructed architecture [vDB11, PvDB12]. In contrast to bottom-up approaches, top-down approaches rely on the existence of a modeled target architecture. Top-down approaches are also known as architecture discovery [DP09].

The calculation of the difference architecture based on a target architecture and the source code is also known as architecture consistency checking [PKB13]. In a study [ABO+17], different ACC approaches from research were compared. The study classified the approaches according to the following characteristics:

- The type of the underlying extraction method (static, dynamic). All approaches of architectural reconstruction use extraction techniques to reveal the relationships between the atomic architectural units (e.g., types, files). Moreover, there is an approach that combines both extraction methods [SSC96]. This approach utilizes information of a dynamic extraction to determine the frequency and, thus, relevance of architecture violations, which are detected based on static extraction.
- The technique for the evaluation of the architectural consistency. Particularly, interesting techniques in this area are:

  – Reflection Modeling (RM) [MNS01], a technique in which source code artifacts are assigned to architectural units of the target architecture. The relationships between modules (actual architecture) are then reconstructed by investigating the relationships of the source code.

- DSL-based approaches [HZ12, GMR15] allow a comfortable definition of the target architecture. In addition to the specification of architectural units and expected relationships, information such as complex conditions for architectural violations or the severity of architectural violations in the event of an occurrence can be defined. DSL-based approaches can be combined with RM-based approaches.

These approaches can also be used for architectures outside the target product. For this purpose, the scope of the relationships under consideration must be extended. In MDD projects, the architecture of the target product as well as the architecture of individual MDD tools, the interaction between tools and artifacts, and the composition of tools into tool chains are of interest for such analyses. In this work, a flexible, RM-based approach for checking architecture consistency for MDD projects is presented. Depending on the application area, static, dynamic, or static and dynamic (in combination) extracted relationship types are considered.

3   Artifact-Based Analysis

This section gives an overview over the developed solution concept to perform artifact-based analyses. Before presenting details, the basic definition of an artifact is given.

Definition 1 An artifact is an individually storable unit with a unique name that serves a specific purpose in the context of the software engineering process.

In this definition, the focus is on the physical manifestation of the artifact rather than on the role in the development process. This requires that an artifact can be stored as an individual unit and then be referenced. Nevertheless, an artifact should serve a defined purpose during the development process because the creation and maintenance of the artifact would otherwise be unnecessary. However, no restrictions are made about how the artifact is integrated into the development process, i.e., an artifact does not necessarily have to describe the target system, for example, in the form of a model, but can also be part of the MDD tool chain instead. The logical content of artifacts thus remains largely unnoticed. This level of abstraction was chosen to effectively analyze the artifact structure, while considering the existing heterogeneous relationships and thus meeting the focus of this work.

An important part of the overall approach is to identify the artifacts, tools, systems, etc., and their relationships present in the system under development. Here, modeling techniques are used, which allow to make these concepts explicit and, thus, enable model-based analyses. Figure 2 gives an overview of the model-based solution concept.

First, it is explicitly defined which types of artifacts, tools, other elements, and relationships in the MDD project under development are of interest. This task will be covered by the architect of the entire MDD project through modeling an artifact model (AM). Such a model structures the corresponding MDD project. As the AM defines the types of elements and relationships and not the concrete instances, this model can stay unchanged over the lifecycle of the entire project unless new artifact or relationship types are added or omitted.

Definition 2 The artifact model defines the relevant artifact types as well as associated relationship types of the MDD project to be examined.

Artifact data reflect the current project state. They can ideally be automatically extracted and stored in one or more artifacts.

Definition 3 Artifact data contain information about the relevant artifacts and their relationships, which are present at a certain point in time in the MDD project. They are defined in conformance to an artifact model.

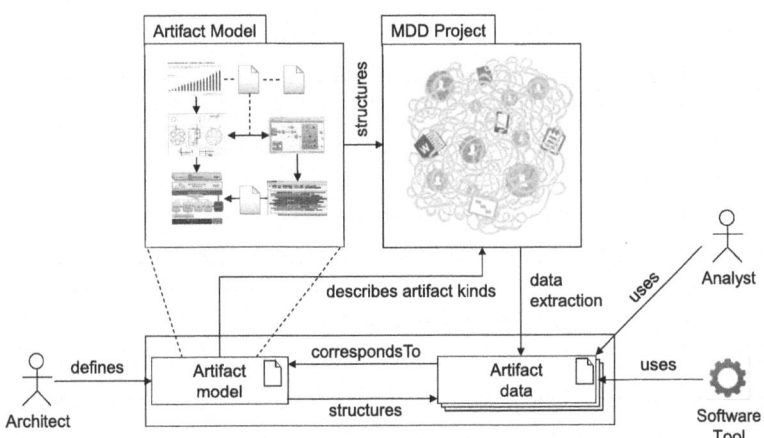

Fig. 2 Solution concept for artifact-based analyses

Artifact data are in an ontological instance relationship [AK03] to the AM, whereby each element and each relationship from the artifact data confirm to an element or relationship type of the AM. Thus, the AM determines the structure of the artifact data. Figure 3 shows how this is reflected in the used modeling technique.

Artifact data represent the project state at a certain point in time. Analysts or special analysis tools can use the extracted artifact data to get an overview of the project state, to check certain relations, create reports, and reveal optimization potential in the project. The overall goal is to make the model-driven development process as efficient as possible.

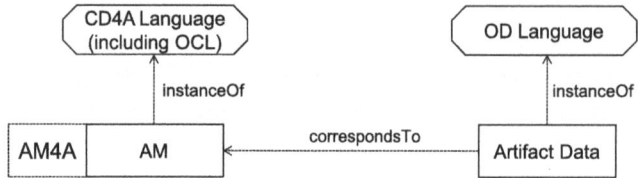

Fig. 3 Overview about the languages and models used for artifact modeling

Beside other kinds of analyses [Gre19], this approach is suited to define and execute architecture consistency checking of model-driven software development projects taking into account input models, MDD tools, which themselves consist of artifacts, and handwritten or generated artifacts that belong to the target product of the development process. A corresponding AM depends on the languages, tools, and technologies used in the project under development. Thus, it must usually be tailored specifically for a given project. However, such a model can be reused as a whole or partially for similar projects.

Fig. 4 Required steps to perform an artifact-based analysis

As shown in Fig. 4, the first step before the execution of artifact-based analysis is to create a project-specific AM. Subsequently, artifact data analyses are specified based on this AM. Based on these two preceding steps, the artifact-based analysis can finally be executed.

3.1 Create Artifact Model

The first step of the methodology is to model an AM. The AM determines the scope for project-specific analyses, explicitly defines the relations between the artifacts, and specifies pre-conditions for the analyses. Furthermore, by using the languages CD and OCL (see Sect. 2.1), it is possible to reuse the existing MDD tools to perform the analyses. An AM core as well as an extensive AM for MontiCore-based MDD projects has already been presented [Gre19]. If a new AM needs to be created or an existing AM needs to be adapted, the AM core and possibly parts of the existing project-specific AMs should be reused. A methodology for this already exists [Gre19].

The central elements of any AM are the artifacts. All project-specific files and folders are considered artifacts. Artifacts can contain each other. Typical examples of artifacts that contain other artifacts are archives or folders of the file system, but database files are also possible. In this paper, we focus on those parts of the AM that are used to perform ACC. Figure 5 shows the relevant part of the AM core.

Since the composite pattern [GHJV95] is used for this part of the AM core, the archives and folders contain each other in any order. Each artifact contained in one artifact container at most. If all available artifacts are modeled, there is exactly one artifact that is not contained in a container: the root directory of the file system. Furthermore, artifacts can contribute to the creation of other artifacts (`produces` relationship), and they can statically reference other artifacts (`refersTo` relationship). These artifact relations are defined as follows:

Definition 4 If an artifact needs information from another artifact to fulfill its purpose, then it refers to the other artifact.

Definition 5 An existing artifact contributes to the creation of the new artifact (to its production) if its existence and/or its contents have an influence on the resulting artifact.

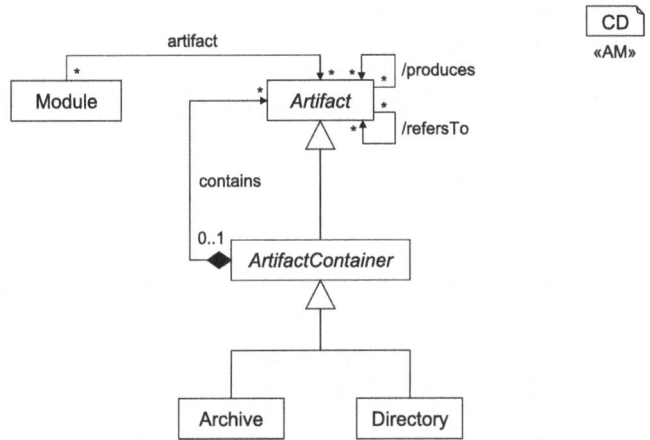

Fig. 5 Part of the AM core relevant for architecture consistency checking

Both relations are defined as derived association in the AM. Thus, these relations must be further specified in project-specific AMs (see Sect. 4), while the definition of artifact data analyses can already be done based on the derived associations (see Sect. 3.4). The specialization of associations is defined using OCL constraints [Gre19], because the CD language does not offer a first class concept here.

Modules represent architectural units based on artifacts and their relationships. The artifacts relation between modules and artifacts must be explicitly defined by the architect. A top-down approach (see Sect. 2.3) is used for the architecture reconstruction part of the analysis.

3.2 Specify Artifact Data Analyses

The second step of the methodology is the specification of project-specific analyses based on the previously created AM. Artifact-based analyses should be repeatable and automated. For this reason, an implementation of the analyses is necessary. This implementation can be either direct in which case the person performing the analysis would have both roles, analyst and analysis tool developer, or the analyst specifies the analyses as requirements for the analysis tool developer, who can then implement a corresponding analysis tool. In this work, analyses are specified using OCL. The reasons for this are:

1. The use of the CD language in the specification of the AM makes it possible to specify analyses using OCL, since the two languages can be used well in combination.
2. The OCL is already used to define project-specific AMs. The reuse of familiar languages reduces the learning curve for analysts, makes analysis specifications readable for architects, and enables reuse in tool development.
3. The OCL has mathematically sound semantics, allowing analyses to be described precisely. OCL expressions are suitable as input for a generator that can automatically convert them into MDD tools. Thus, this tool implementation step can be automated, reducing the effort for the analysis tool developer.

As this paper focuses on ACC, Sect. 2.3 defines architecture consistency checking as artifact data analysis in detail. Other kinds of artifact-based analyses are presented in the original thesis [Gre19].

3.3 Artifact-Based Analyses

As third step of Fig. 4, the artifact-based analysis is executed. This step is divided into five sub-steps, which are supported by automated and reusable tooling. Figure 6 shows these steps and their corresponding tools.

When performing artifact-based analyses, the first step is the extraction of relevant project data. If the data are stored in different files, a merge of the data takes place. The entire data set is then checked for conformity to the AM. In the next step, the data are accumulated based on the specification of the AM, so that the derived properties are present when performing the last step, the artifact data analysis. To support the steps of performing analyses, the MontiCore Artifact Toolchain (MontiArT) was developed [Gre19]. MontiArT is a tool chain that can be used to collect, merge, validate, accumulate, and finally analyze artifact data. Thus, all sub-steps of the artifact-based analysis are supported. The individual steps are each performed by one or more small tools, which can be combined in a tool chain, for example, by using a script. The tools shown in Fig. 6 are arranged according to the tool chain's execution order. The architecture as tool chain is modular and

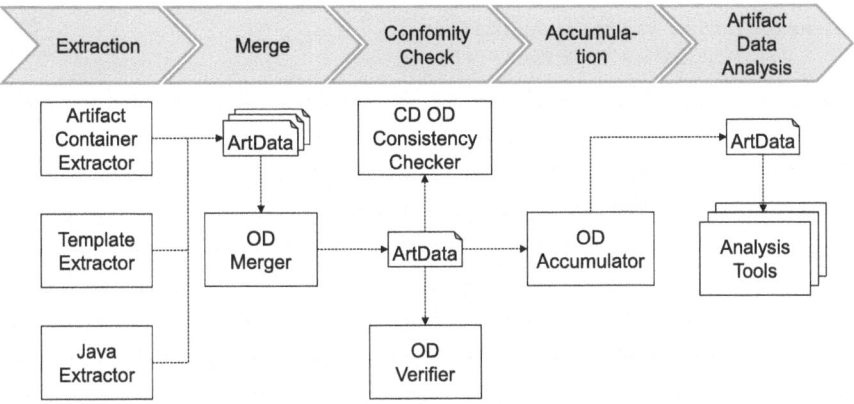

Fig. 6 Sub-step of the artifact-based analysis

adaptable. New tools can be added without the need to adapt other tools. Existing tools can be adapted or removed from the tool chain without having to adapt other tools. This is advantageous, since this work is based on the assumption that there is no universal AM for all MDD projects [Gre19]. For this reason, when using the tool chain in a new project, it is usually necessary to make project-specific adjustments. The selected architecture supports the reuse and adjustments of individual tools.

3.4   Artifact-Based Analysis for Architecture Consistency Checking

In architecture reconstruction (see Sect. 2.3), the relationships between the architectural units of the system are reconstructed, which are represented here by modules (see Sect. 3.3). Modules can be defined for the models and tools used in the project as well as for the product to be developed. By explicitly modeling modules and assigning artifacts of the project to modules, an abstract project view can be created that gives stakeholders (architects, developers, or tool developers) a good overview of the MDD project. Modules can often be identified by the existing packages or folders. However, due to architectural erosion (see Sect. 2.3), this alignment can be lost. It is also possible to define different architectures for a single project, each with a different focus [Lil16]. Furthermore, different types of modules can generally be defined for predefined elements of a software architecture, such as components, layers, or interfaces. In general, it is recommended that the specified modules are reflected as well as possible by an appropriate structure in the project. The relationships between modules can be derived based on the assigned artifacts as shown in Listing 2.

```
 1   association /containedArtifact                                    CD
 2      [*] Module -> Artifact [*];                                   «AM4A»
 3
 4   context Module m, ArtfiactContainer c inv:
 5      m.containedArtifact.containsAll(m.artifact) &&
 6      m.artifact.contains(c) implies m.artifact.containsAll(c.
              contains**);
 7
 8   association /externalReferredArtifact
 9      [*] Module -> Artifact [*];
10   association /externalProducedArtifact
11      [*] Module -> Artifact [*];
12
13   context Module inv: (*@ \label{1st:applications_module:
              reliesonartifacts} @*)
14      externalReferredArtifact ==
15        containedArtifact.refersTo.removeAll(containedArtifact);
16
17   context Module inv: (*@ \label{1st:applications_module:
              producedartifact} @*)
18      externalProducedArtifact ==
19        containedArtifact.produces.removeAll(containedArtifact);
20
21   association /reliesOnModule [*] Module -> Module [*];
22   association /contributionModule [*] Module -> Module [*];
23
24   context Module inv: (*@ \label{1st:applications_module:
              reliesonmodules} @*)
25      reliesOnModule == externalReferredArtifact.module;
26
27   context Module inv: (*@ \label{1st:applications_module:
              contributionmodule} @*)
28      contributionModule == externalProducedArtifact.module;
```

Listing 2 Specification of the artifact data analysis for architecture consistency checking: actual architecture

A distinction is made between two different types of module relationships, which can be calculated based on the assigned artifacts and their relationships. The reliesOnModule relationship indicates that a module refers to another module, while the contributionModule relationship indicates the participation of a module in the creation of another module similar to the corresponding relations for artifacts defined in Sect. 3.1. To calculate the relationships, further derived auxiliary associations were defined. Each module can contain a set of artifacts, which is defined as the set of artifacts directly assigned to the module together with all artifacts transitively contained by assigned artifacts. Thus, when assigning a folder to a module, contained artifacts are also regarded to be part of that module. Furthermore, for each module, the external artifacts can be calculated, which are those artifacts that are related to artifacts of the module, but are not assigned to the module themselves. Depending on the type of the underlying artifact relationship, the relationship is represented by the `externalReferredArtifact` or the `externalProducedArtifact` relationship in the shown AM extension. With the help of these associations, the calculations of `reliesOnModule` and `contributionModule` are specified, which results in the actual architecture of the system under development.

Based on the actual architecture, the difference architecture between the target and the actual architecture can also be calculated with the help of an AM extension. The first required extension part for this analysis is shown in Listing 3. It allows the specification of the target architecture.

```
29   association intendedReference [*] Module -> Module [*];    CD
30   association intendedContribution
31     [*] Module -> Module [*];                               «AM4A»
```

Listing 3 Specification of the artifact data analysis for architecture consistency checking: target architecture

With the help of the two associations `intendedReference` and `intended-Contribution`, the intended relationships between modules can be specified. These can then be used to calculate the differences between the target and actual architecture. The second extension part for this analysis is shown in Listing 4. It allows the representation of the difference architecture and specifies its calculation.

```
32   association /unintendedReference                          CD
33     [*] Module -> Module [*];
34   association /unintendedContribution                       «AM4A»
35     [*] Module -> Module [*];
36
37   association /missingReference [*] Module -> Module [*];
38   association /missingContribution [*] Module -> Module [*];
39
40   context Module inv:
41     unintendedReference ==
42       reliesOnModule.removeAll(intendedReference);
43
44   context Module inv:
45     unintendedContribution ==
46       contributionModule.removeAll(intendedContribution);
47
48   context Module inv:
49     missingReference ==
50       intendedReference.removeAll(reliesOnModule);
51
52   context Module inv:
53     missingContribution ==
54       intendedContribution.removeAll(contributionModule);
```

Listing 4 Specification of the artifact data analysis for architecture consistency checking: difference architecture

To be able to capture the results of the calculations, four derived associations were introduced. For each type of relationship to be compared, two associations are specified here. One represents the unexpected, additional relationships of the actual architecture in comparison to the target architecture, and the other contains the missing, but intended relationships. The unintended, additional relationships can be calculated by removing the intended relationships from the set of existing relationships. In contrast to this, missing, intended relationships can be calculated by removing the existing relationships from the set of intended relationships.

4   Applied Analyses

This section describes two different applied artifact-based analyses for architecture consistency checking. For both analyses, only step one (*Create Artifact Model*) and step three (*Artifact-based Analysis*) are described. Step two (*Specify Artifact Data Analyses*) was already presented in Sect. 3.4. As the defined analysis works completely on the concepts of the presented AM core, there is no need to define different analyses for the two different applications.

4.1   DEx Generator

The MontiCore Data Explorer (DEx) [Rot17] is a generator based on MontiCore that transforms an input CD into an executable system for data exploration. In addition to the generation of data classes, a graphical user interface and a persistence layer to connect the application to a database can be generated.

DEx offers a mechanism for the integration of handwritten code and a mechanism for the exchange and addition of templates by the generator user making the generator very flexible and the generation process highly configurable. Furthermore, internal M2M transformations take place when the generator is executed. The configuration functionality and the execution of internal model transformations lead to the fact that generation processes in different DEx-based development projects can differ greatly. For this reason, an analysis of DEx-based projects is particularly interesting.

DEx is delivered together with an exemplary CD model for generating an application for a social network. A target architecture was created together with the architect of DEx using the exemplary CD model as input for the generator. The architecture consists of eleven modules, which can be part of the generator, the generated product, or the runtime environment. As preparation for the analysis, the project-specific AM shown in Figs. 7 and 8 was modeled.

Figure 7 presents the project-specific refersTo relations of the DEx generator. The reflexive reliesOnJavaArtifact association indicates that two Java artifacts are dependent on each other. One Java source code file is dependent on

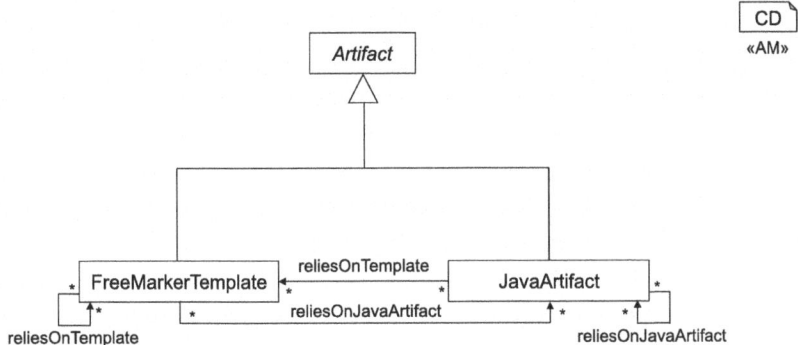

Fig. 7 Specific `refersTo` relationships between template and Java artifacts in the DEx project

another Java artifact iff the other artifact must be loaded when compiling the source code file. A .class file depends on another artifact iff something (type, method, constant, . . .) from the other file is used when executing the part of the program defined by the .class file.

Templates can call each other during their execution [Sch12], which means that templates are dependent on other templates. This relationship is modeled by the `reliesOnTemplate` relationship of the AM. Furthermore, it is possible to create Java objects from templates and to store them temporarily, provide them as parameters to other templates, and call their methods. Hence, templates can depend on the existence of the corresponding Java artifacts. This relationship is represented by the `reliesOnJavaArtifact` relationship. Java artifacts can rely on the existence of templates when replacing standard templates with project-specific templates [Rot17].

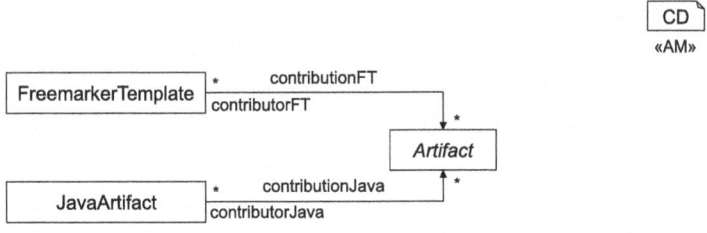

Fig. 8 Template and Java artifacts contribute to the creation of artifacts

The relationships `contributionFT` and `contributionJava` are specializations of the produces relation. Whenever a Java or template artifact of the generator contributes to the generation of a target file, such a relation is recorded in the artifact data.

To extract the data of the shown AM, several reusable as well as project-specific extractors were used. In the following step, the artifact data of each extractor are merged into a single artifact data file, which acts as the first input for the calculation of the actual architecture. The second input for the calculation of the actual architecture is the module definition, i.e., the assignment of artifacts to the modules of the target architecture defined by the project's architect. Based on the calculated actual architecture and the modeled target architecture, the difference architecture of the DEx project was determined, which is shown in Fig. 9.

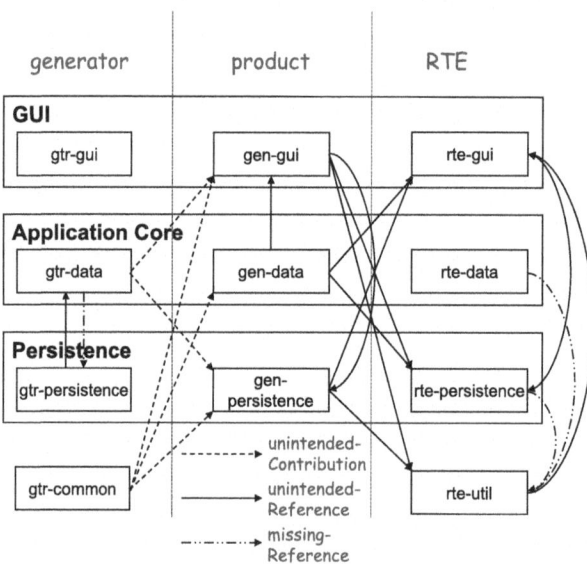

Fig. 9 Result of the artifact-based analysis: The difference architecture of the DEx project

The number of relationships present in the difference architecture reveals that a major architectural degradation has occurred. An architectural degradation leads to the fact that per time unit less and less functionality can be implemented and bugs can be fixed, which ultimately leads to frustrated and demotivated developers [Lil16]. Based on the analysis performed, the revealed architecture degradation can be eliminated, thus counteracting these problems. For this purpose, it must be decided individually for each relationship whether it is a violation of the target architecture or whether the target architecture is outdated at this point. The cause for unwanted relationships of the difference architecture can be traced using reporting files created as by-product by the tooling. To update an outdated target architecture, missing required relationships must be added and required relationships that have become obsolete must be removed. In the case that the target architecture is still valid, the corresponding relationship indicates a problem in the source code of the project. When remedying such a problem, missing and additional, unintended relationships of the actual architecture must be treated differently. Unintended

Table 1 Examined artifacts of the DEx project

Module	JavaSourceFile	FreeMarkerTemplate	$\sum$
gtr-gui	19	96	115
gtr-data	27	92	119
gtr-persistence	14	93	107
gtr-commons	17	5	22
gen-gui	121	0	121
gen-data	44	0	44
gen-persistence	121	0	121
rte-gui	119	0	119
rte-data	10	0	10
rte-persistence	17	0	17
rte-util	8	0	8
Nicht zugewiesen	38	15	53
$\sum$	555	301	856

Table 2 Examined relations between artifacts of the DEx project

Relation	Source artifact	Amount
contains	Directory	940
imports	JavaSourceFile	1815
reliesOnJava	JavaSourceFile	3807
reliesOnTemplate	JavaSourceFile	324
reliesOnJava	FreeMarkerTemplate	88
reliesOnTemplate	FreeMarkerTemplate	59
contributionJava	JavaSourceFile	270
contributionFT	FreeMarkerTemplate	2760
$\sum$		10,063

relationships must be eliminated by refactoring the source code in any case, while a missing relationships can be either also fixed by a refactoring or it indicates that the desired, corresponding functionality was not implemented at all or in a fundamentally different way.

Finally, Tables 1 and 2 summarize some numbers to give an impression of the scope of the project and the regarded artifact and relationship types.

4.2 MontiCar Repositories

While the artifact-based analysis of DEx focuses on a single development project, we also applied our methodology to multiple projects located in different repositories. Although these projects reside in different locations, i.e., version control repositories, they are still related to each other. More specifically, our goal was to perform architectural compliance checking for the MontiCar family, a family of projects developed in the context of autonomous driving and other automotive related topics [KRRvW17, KRSvW18, KNP+19].

In case of multiple projects, we change our approach in such a way that we define modules for the architectural compliance check based on the projects rather than single parts of each project. For example, the project containing common functionality for all other projects forms a single module or all functionality used for visualization purposes is comprised in a single module. Next, the target architecture for the set of projects is defined. Listing 5 shows an excerpt of this definition.

The *EmbeddedMontiArc* module has an intended relation to the commons and visualization modules as well as to the *EmbeddedMontiArcView* module. For the analyses of the MontiCar family, in general, we used the same specifications as defined for DEx in Listings 2, 3, and 4. Furthermore, we assigned the *src* folder of each project to the respective module since each project is a Maven project. The transitive closure of the *src* folder defined the set of artifacts considered for the ACC as described in Listing 2, ll. 3-5.

For the analysis of MontiCar, we only considered intended references between the modules, since contribute relations only exist within each project. The primary goals were to first check if all intended relations between modules actually exist and second to get an overview of all unintended relations within the family. With the help of the respective results, we then improved the current architecture of the family to adhere to the target architecture.

```
 1 objectdiagram ModuleRelations {                                    OD
 2                                                                    «MD»
 3   EmbeddedMontiArc:Module{};
 4   EmbeddedMontiView:Module{};
 5   languagescommon:Module{};
 6   visualisation:Module{};
 7
 8
 9   link intendedReference EmbeddedMontiArc -> EmbeddedMontiView;
10   link intendedReference EmbeddedMontiArc -> languagescommon;
11   link intendedReference EmbeddedMontiArc -> visualisation;
12 }
```

Listing 5 Excerpt of the module definition for the MontiCar project family

Table 3 shows the results of the ACC for the MontiCar family. The first column displays the defined modules, and the following columns contain the total number of artifacts analyzed, the number of intended references for each module defined in the target architecture, and the found numbers of unintended and missing references as part of the difference architecture. Looking at the results, it is interesting to see that for most of the modules either a unintended or missing reference was discovered. Moreover, the analysis found unintended references for more than half of the modules. Unintended references are references not contained in the target

Table 3 Results of analysis containing the number of artifacts of each module, the number of intended references of the target architecture, the number of unintended references, and the number of missing references

Module	# Artifacts	# Intended	# Unintended	# Missing
EmbeddedMontiArc	151	6	0	1
Enum	110	0	3	0
languagescommon	136	0	3	0
EmbeddedMontiArcMath	261	4	2	0
MontiMath	119	5	1	1
TaggingExamples	31	2	2	0
Struct	51	4	0	0
EmbeddedMontiView	120	4	2	2
EMAM2Cpp	357	9	1	0
ViewVerification	181	5	2	0
reporting	510	4	1	1
Tagging	121	1	0	0
NumberUnit	26	1	0	0
visualisation	188	6	3	3
$\sum$	2362	51	20	8

architecture, however, present in the actual architecture. In general, these deviations illustrate the architectural erosion within the MontiCar family. Depending on the module, one deviation is considered more critical than others. For example, for the *languagescommon* project, the number of intended references is zero, since it contains common functionality, which must not relate to any other project. However, three unintended references to other projects of the family were found. The impact of other occurrences in the difference architecture is less critical, since these were classified as architectural drift. Especially, missing references between modules fall into this category for the MontiCar project. As a consequence, the target architecture was adjusted in these cases accordingly.

Using the results of the artifact-based analysis, we were able to look at each of the references found in the current state of the MontiCar family in more detail. Besides currently existing references between modules, the analysis also provided a detailed list of the artifacts and their relations that cause a reference between modules. For each of the unintended module references not contained in the target architecture, we had the options to reduce the architectural drift:

- Declare the reference to be unintended and as a consequence refactor the artifacts causing the reference.
- Declare the reference to be intended and add it to the target architecture.

Finally, we were able to reduce the architectural drift within the family of projects using the artifact-based architectural consistency checking and continue to perform it regularly to keep the architectural drift as small as possible at all times.

5 Conclusion

MDD helps to master the complexity of software development and to reduce the conceptual gap between the problem and the solution domain. By using models and MDD tools, the software development process can be at least partially automated. Especially when MDD techniques are used in large development projects, it can be difficult to manage the huge number of different artifacts, different artifact kinds, and MDD tools. This can lead to poor maintainability or an inefficient build process. The goal of the presented approach is the development of concepts, methods, and tools for artifact-based analysis of model-driven software development projects. The term artifact-based analysis is used to describe a reverse engineering methodology, which enables repeatable and automated analyses of artifact structures. To describe artifacts and their relationships, artifact and relationship types, and for the specification of analyses, a UML/P-based modeling technique was developed. This enables the specification of project-specific artifact models via CD and OCL parts. As part of the modeling technique, a reusable AM core is defined. In addition, analysis specifications can also be defined by CDs and OCL, while artifact data that represent the current project situation are defined by ODs. The choice of modeling technique allows you to check the consistency between an AM and artifact data. The models are specified in a human readable form but can also be automatically processed by MDD tools. The artifact-based analysis consists of five sub-steps, which, starting from an MDD project and an associated AM, allows the execution of specified analyses.

While this paper gave an overview of the contributions of the original thesis [Gre19], not all contributions could be covered in detail. Especially, this paper focused on only a single kind of artifact-based analysis, architecture consistency checking, whereas the original thesis presents several different analysis kinds. Moreover, Sect. 4.2 of this work described an additional case of application succeeding the former work.

Due to the results obtained, this work contributes to handling the increasing complexity of large MDD projects by explicit modeling artifact and relationship types, which can be used for manual and automated analysis of MDD projects. Hidden relationships can be revealed and checked immediately, which opens up the possibility for corrections and optimizations in a given project.

References

ABO+17. Nour Ali, Sean Baker, Ross O'Crowley, Sebastian Herold, and Jim Buckley. Architecture consistency: State of the practice, challenges and requirements. *Empirical Software Engineering*, pages 1–35, 2017.

AHRW17. Kai Adam, Katrin Hölldobler, Bernhard Rumpe, and Andreas Wortmann. Engineering Robotics Software Architectures with Exchangeable Model Transformations. In *International Conference on Robotic Computing (IRC'17)*, pages 172–179. IEEE, April 2017.

AIM10. Luigi Atzori, Antonio Iera, and Giacomo Morabito. The Internet of Things: A survey. *Computer Networks*, 54:2787–2805, 2010.

AK03. C. Atkinson and T. Kuhne. Model-Driven Development: A Metamodeling Foundation. *IEEE Software*, 20:36–41, 2003.

BCW12. Marco Brambilla, Jordi Cabot, and Manuel Wimmer. *Model-Driven Software Engineering in Practice*. Morgan & Claypool Publishers, 2012.

CCF⁺15. Betty H. C. Cheng, Benoit Combemale, Robert B. France, Jean-Marc Jézéquel, and Bernhard Rumpe. On the Globalization of Domain Specific Languages. In *Globalizing Domain-Specific Languages*, LNCS 9400, pages 1–6. Springer, 2015.

DP09. Stephane Ducasse and Damien Pollet. Software Architecture Reconstruction: A Process-Oriented Taxonomy. *IEEE Transactions on Software Engineering*, 35:573–591, 2009.

EF17. C. Ebert and J. Favaro. Automotive Software. *IEEE Software*, 34:33–39, 2017.

FR07. Robert France and Bernhard Rumpe. Model-driven Development of Complex Software: A Research Roadmap. *Future of Software Engineering (FOSE '07)*, pages 37–54, May 2007.

GHJV95. Erich Gamma, Richard Helm, Ralph Johnson, and John Vlissides. *Design Patterns: Elements of Reusable Object-Oriented Software*. Addison-Wesley, 1995.

GHR17. Timo Greifenberg, Steffen Hillemacher, and Bernhard Rumpe. *Towards a Sustainable Artifact Model: Artifacts in Generator-Based Model-Driven Projects*. Aachener Informatik-Berichte, Software Engineering, Band 30. Shaker Verlag, December 2017.

GIM13. Joshua Garcia, Igor Ivkovic, and Nenad Medvidovic. A Comparative Analysis of Software Architecture Recovery Techniques. In *Proceedings of the 28th IEEE/ACM International Conference on Automated Software Engineering*, pages 486–496. IEEE Press, 2013.

GKR⁺06. Hans Grönniger, Holger Krahn, Bernhard Rumpe, Martin Schindler, and Steven Völkel. MontiCore 1.0 - Ein Framework zur Erstellung und Verarbeitung domänenspezifischer Sprachen. Informatik-Bericht 2006-04, CFG-Fakultät, TU Braunschweig, August 2006.

GKR⁺08. Hans Grönniger, Holger Krahn, Bernhard Rumpe, Martin Schindler, and Steven Völkel. MontiCore: A Framework for the Development of Textual Domain Specific Languages. In *30th International Conference on Software Engineering (ICSE 2008), Leipzig, Germany, May 10–18, 2008, Companion Volume*, pages 925–926, 2008.

GMR15. Timo Greifenberg, Klaus Müller, and Bernhard Rumpe. Architectural Consistency Checking in Plugin-Based Software Systems. In *European Conference on Software Architecture Workshops (ECSAW'15)*, pages 58:1–58:7. ACM, 2015.

Gre19. Timo Greifenberg. *Artefaktbasierte Analyse modellgetriebener Softwareentwicklungsprojekte*. Aachener Informatik-Berichte, Software Engineering, Band 42. Shaker Verlag, August 2019.

Höl18. Katrin Hölldobler. *MontiTrans: Agile, modellgetriebene Entwicklung von und mit domänenspezifischen, kompositionalen Transformationssprachen*. Aachener Informatik-Berichte, Software Engineering, Band 36. Shaker Verlag, December 2018.

HR17. Katrin Hölldobler and Bernhard Rumpe. *MontiCore 5 Language Workbench Edition 2017*. Aachener Informatik-Berichte, Software Engineering, Band 32. Shaker Verlag, December 2017.

HRW15. Katrin Hölldobler, Bernhard Rumpe, and Ingo Weisemöller. Systematically Deriving Domain-Specific Transformation Languages. In *Conference on Model Driven Engineering Languages and Systems (MODELS'15)*, pages 136–145. ACM/IEEE, 2015.

HZ12. Thomas Haitzer and Uwe Zdun. DSL-based Support for Semi-automated Architectural Component Model Abstraction Throughout the Software Lifecycle. In *Proceedings of the 8th International ACM SIGSOFT Conference on Quality of Software Architectures*, QoSA '12. ACM, 2012.

Jac11. Daniel Jackson. *Software Abstractions: Logic, Language, and Analysis*. MIT press, 2011.

KNP+19. Evgeny Kusmenko, Sebastian Nickels, Svetlana Pavlitskaya, Bernhard Rumpe, and Thomas Timmermanns. Modeling and Training of Neural Processing Systems. In Marouane Kessentini, Tao Yue, Alexander Pretschner, Sebastian Voss, and Loli Burgueño, editors, *Conference on Model Driven Engineering Languages and Systems (MODELS'19)*, pages 283–293. IEEE, September 2019.

Kra10. Holger Krahn. *MontiCore: Agile Entwicklung von domänenspezifischen Sprachen im Software-Engineering*. Aachener Informatik-Berichte, Software Engineering, Band 1. Shaker Verlag, März 2010.

KRR14. Helmut Krcmar, Ralf Reussner, and Bernhard Rumpe. *Trusted Cloud Computing*. Springer, Schweiz, December 2014.

KRRvW17. Evgeny Kusmenko, Alexander Roth, Bernhard Rumpe, and Michael von Wenckstern. Modeling Architectures of Cyber-Physical Systems. In *European Conference on Modelling Foundations and Applications (ECMFA'17)*, LNCS 10376, pages 34–50. Springer, July 2017.

KRSvW18. Evgeny Kusmenko, Bernhard Rumpe, Sascha Schneiders, and Michael von Wenckstern. Highly-Optimizing and Multi-Target Compiler for Embedded System Models: C++ Compiler Toolchain for the Component and Connector Language Embedded-MontiArc. In *Conference on Model Driven Engineering Languages and Systems (MODELS'18)*, pages 447–457. ACM, October 2018.

KRV08. Holger Krahn, Bernhard Rumpe, and Steven Völkel. Monticore: Modular Development of Textual Domain Specific Languages. In *Conference on Objects, Models, Components, Patterns (TOOLS-Europe'08)*, LNBIP 11, pages 297–315. Springer, 2008.

KRV10. Holger Krahn, Bernhard Rumpe, and Stefen Völkel. MontiCore: a Framework for Compositional Development of Domain Specific Languages. *International Journal on Software Tools for Technology Transfer (STTT)*, 12(5):353–372, September 2010.

Lee08. Edward A. Lee. Cyber Physical Systems: Design Challenges. In *2008 11th IEEE International Symposium on Object and Component-Oriented Real-Time Distributed Computing (ISORC)*, pages 363–369, 2008.

Lil16. Carola Lilienthal. *Langlebige Software-Architekturen: Technische Schulden analysieren, begrenzen und abbauen*. dpunkt, 2016.

MHDZ16. Markus Müller, Klaus Hörmann, Lars Dittmann, and Jörg Zimmer. *Automotive SPICE in der Praxis: Interpretationshilfe für Anwender und Assessoren*. dpunkt.verlag, 2 edition, 2016.

MNS01. G. C. Murphy, D. Notkin, and K. J. Sullivan. Software Reflexion Models: Bridging the Gap between Design and Implementation. *IEEE Transactions on Software Engineering*, 27:364–380, 2001.

MRR11. Shahar Maoz, Jan Oliver Ringert, and Bernhard Rumpe. An Operational Semantics for Activity Diagrams using SMV. Technical Report AIB-2011-07, RWTH Aachen University, Aachen, Germany, July 2011.

NPR13. Antonio Navarro Pérez and Bernhard Rumpe. Modeling Cloud Architectures as Interactive Systems. In *Model-Driven Engineering for High Performance and Cloud Computing Workshop*, volume 1118 of *CEUR Workshop Proceedings*, pages 15–24, 2013.

OMG14. Object Management Group. Object Constraint Language (OCL, 2014. http://www.omg.org/spec/OCL/2.4.

OMG15. Object Management Group. Unified Modeling Language (UML), 2015. http://www.omg.org/spec/UML/.

OMG17. Object Management Group. OMG Systems Modeling Language (OMG SysML), 2017. http://www.omg.org/spec/SysML/1.5/.

PKB13. L. Pruijt, C. Köppe, and S. Brinkkemper. Architecture Compliance Checking of Semantically Rich Modular Architectures: A Comparative Study of Tool Support. In *2013 IEEE International Conference on Software Maintenance*, 2013.

PvDB12. M. C. Platenius, M. von Detten, and S. Becker. Archimetrix: Improved Software Architecture Recovery in the Presence of Design Deficiencies. In *2012 16th European Conference on Software Maintenance and Reengineering*, pages 255–264, 2012.

Rot17. Alexander Roth. *Adaptable Code Generation of Consistent and Customizable Data Centric Applications with MontiDex*. Aachener Informatik-Berichte, Software Engineering, Band 31. Shaker Verlag, December 2017.

RSW+15. Bernhard Rumpe, Christoph Schulze, Michael von Wenckstern, Jan Oliver Ringert, and Peter Manhart. Behavioral Compatibility of Simulink Models for Product Line Maintenance and Evolution. In *Software Product Line Conference (SPLC'15)*, pages 141–150. ACM, 2015.

Rum16. Bernhard Rumpe. *Modeling with UML: Language, Concepts, Methods*. Springer International, July 2016.

Rum17. Bernhard Rumpe. *Agile Modeling with UML: Code Generation, Testing, Refactoring*. Springer International, May 2017.

Sch12. Martin Schindler. *Eine Werkzeuginfrastruktur zur agilen Entwicklung mit der UML/P*. Aachener Informatik-Berichte, Software Engineering, Band 11. Shaker Verlag, 2012.

SSC96. Mohlalefi Sefika, Aamod Sane, and Roy H. Campbell. Monitoring Compliance of a Software System with Its High-level Design Models. In *Proceedings of the 18th International Conference on Software Engineering*, ICSE '96, pages 387–396. IEEE Computer Society, 1996.

TMD09. R. N. Taylor, N. Medvidovic, and E. M. Dashofy. *Software Architecture: Foundations, Theory, and Practice*. Wiley, 2009.

vDB11. Markus von Detten and Steffen Becker. Combining Clustering and Pattern Detection for the Reengineering of Component-based Software Systems. In *Proceedings of the Joint ACM SIGSOFT Conference – QoSA and ACM SIGSOFT Symposium – ISARCS on Quality of Software Architectures – QoSA and Architecting Critical Systems – ISARCS*, QoSA-ISARCS '11, pages 23–32. ACM, 2011.

Völ11. Steven Völkel. *Kompositionale Entwicklung domänenspezifischer Sprachen*. Aachener Informatik-Berichte, Software Engineering, Band 9. Shaker Verlag, 2011.

Wei12. Ingo Weisemöller. *Generierung domänenspezifischer Transformationssprachen*. Aachener Informatik-Berichte, Software Engineering, Band 12. Shaker Verlag, 2012.

WHR14. J. Whittle, J. Hutchinson, and M. Rouncefield. The state of practice in model-driven engineering. *IEEE Software*, 31(3):79–85, 2014.

Same but Different: Consistently Developing and Evolving Software Architecture Models and Their Implementation

Marco Konersmann and Michael Goedicke

Abstract As software architecture is a main driver for the software quality, source code is often accompanied by software architecture specifications. When the implementation is changed, the architecture specification is often not updated along with the code, which introduces inconsistencies between these artifacts. Such inconsistencies imply a risk of misunderstandings and errors during the development, maintenance, and evolution, causing serious degradation over the lifetime of the system. In this chapter we present the Explicitly Integrated Architecture approach and its tool *Codeling*, which remove the necessity for a separate representation of software architecture by integrating software architecture information with the program code. By using our approach, the specification can be extracted from the source code and changes in the specification can be propagated to the code. The integration of architecture information with the code leaves no room for inconsistencies between the artifacts and creates links between artifacts. We evaluate the approach and tool in a use case with real software in development and with a benchmark software, accompanied by a performance evaluation.

1 Introduction

In the development of software systems, the software architecture [32] describes the software's general building blocks, including structural and behavioral aspects. Software architecture is one of the main drivers for software quality. Due to its importance, software architecture is often modeled in some way, for communicating and analyzing the architecture. This includes a brief sketch on a sheet of paper and goes up to extensive specifications in formal languages.

M. Konersmann (✉)
University of Koblenz-Landau, Mainz, Germany
e-mail: konersmann@uni-koblenz.de

M. Goedicke
University of Duisburg-Essen, Duisburg, Germany
e-mail: michael.goedicke@paluno.uni-due.de

M. Felderer et al. (eds.), *Ernst Denert Award for Software Engineering 2019*,
https://doi.org/10.1007/978-3-030-58617-1_6

87

While the software architecture can be modeled, it certainly will be implemented using programming languages to build an executable system. The current major programming languages, such as Java, C, Python, and so on [1], do not provide abstractions for components and connectors. A translation between the concepts of architecture specification languages and programming languages is required for a project, to understand how these concepts are implemented. Developers either create project-specific conventions to implement architectural features or use one of many component implementation frameworks. Components are then, e.g., implemented by a class definition with a name ending with Component within a package. The component provides interfaces by implementing a corresponding interface, that is defined in the same package. Conventions like these can be found in many software systems, often not even documented. Implementation frameworks specify recurring patterns for implementing architecture information such as component-based structures. For example, in Enterprise Java Beans (EJB) [23] Java classes with specific annotations can be used as components.

Both, conventions and frameworks, can be seen as architecture implementation languages. They consider program code to describe architectural information. But a program is not complete with an architecture alone. Further program code is necessary to implement the detailed behavior or fine-grained structures, which is required to build an executable and functional system. Architecture implementation languages also need to provide room for such program code.

Languages for specifying and for implementing software architectures share a common core: components and their interconnection [22]. As they describe overlapping information, they should be consistent. Undetected inconsistencies may be the source for misunderstandings and errors in the implementation. Automated consistency checks can identify whether an architecture specification and its implementation are in a consistent state. Existing approaches for consistency of architecture models and implementations usually focus on a pair of specification and implementation languages (see related work in Sect. 5). New approaches need to be developed for emerging or evolving languages, which take the specific features of the languages into account and respect existing, non-architectural program code.

A variety of software architecture specification languages exist, such as dedicated architecture description languages (ADLs) [18] or general-purpose modeling languages, that are feasible to describe software architectures, such as the Unified Modeling Language (UML). The different languages provide different features, including component hierarchies, different types of connectors, or different concepts of abstract behavior. The implementation of software architecture is similarly diverse. This diversity is a challenge for maintaining the consistency of architecture implementations and specifications.

This chapter presents the following main contributions:

1. The *Explicitly Integrated Architecture* (EIA) approach automatically maintains the consistency of implemented and specified architectures. It translates between program code and architecture models, by extracting architecture models from code and propagating model changes back to the code. It takes the difference of

architecture languages into account and reduces the effort for integrating new or evolved languages into the architecture model/code translation.

2. The *Model Integration Concept* is an approach for translating between program code and software design models using translation patterns.
3. The *Intermediate Architecture Description Language* is an intermediate language to translate between different software architecture languages.
4. *Architecture Model Transformations* based on the Intermediate Architecture Description Language translate between software architecture languages.
5. The tool *Codeling*[1] implements the EIA approach and has been used for evaluation in synthetic and real environments.
6. A *code generation tool* generates concrete model/code translations from translation patterns.

We will present our approach as follows: In Sect. 2 we present our approach. Codeling is presented in Sect. 3. We describe the evaluation and discuss its results in Sect. 4. Related work is presented in Sect. 5, before we conclude in Sect. 6 and present the future work.

2 The Explicitly Integrated Architecture Approach

The *Explicitly Integrated Architecture (EIA)* approach extracts architecture models from code and propagates model changes back to the code. Using the proposed approach, architecture model information is integrated with program code. The code will be structured in a way that architecture meta model and model elements and their properties can reliably be extracted and changed. Non-architectural code is not overwritten when model changes are propagated.

Figure 1 sketches an overview of the approach. Artifacts of the approach are represented with rounded boxes and translations between these artifacts with arrows. The parts of the approach are used to bidirectionally translate between program code and a specification model expressed in an architecture specification language. They are underlined in Fig. 1.

1. *Program Code:* the implementation of a software following the standards of an architecture implementation language
2. *Implementation Model:* an abstract model view upon the program code, which complies to an architecture implementation language
3. *Translation Model:* an intermediate model view for translating between an implementation model and a specification model
4. *Specification Model:* a specification of architectural concerns using an architecture specification language

---

[1]The tool *Codeling* and its accompanying code generator are available at https://codeling.de as open source, licensed EPL 1.0.

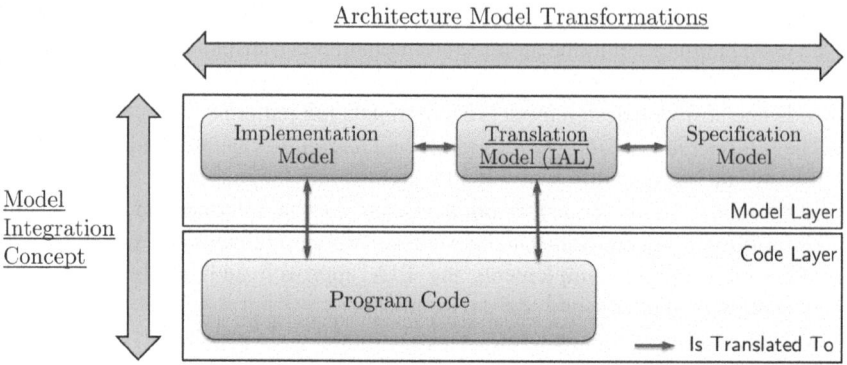

Fig. 1 The view types of the EIA approach and the means to translate between them (underlined)

The EIA is comprised of four parts:

1. The **Model Integration Concept** integrates models and meta models with program code. It is used to create well-defined translations between program code structures, model elements, and meta model elements. It extracts arbitrary design models from code and propagates changes in the models to the code again.
2. The translation model reduces the number of translation definitions required between architecture implementation and specification model languages. We define the **Intermediate Architecture Description Language (IAL)** to express translation models.
3. **Architecture Model Transformations** are used for the translation between models of different languages and for transformations within models of the IAL.
4. The **Explicitly Integrated Architecture Process** describes how these areas are used to achieve the overall objective.

While the Model Integration Concept would suffice for extracting architecture models from code, it does not provide the necessary flexibility to handle new and evolving languages with different features. The IAL and the transformations are required to fulfill these objectives.

2.1 Explicitly Integrated Architecture Process

The Explicitly Integrated Architecture Process [11] is visualized in Fig. 2. It starts from program code that complies to an implementation model, including code that has not been developed using the process yet. An empty code base can also be a start for green field development. The process defines three main steps for each direction. For extracting a specification model, the following steps are executed:

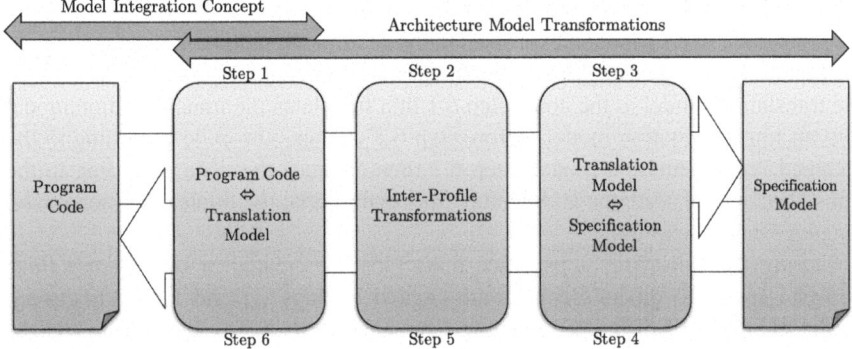

Fig. 2 Overview of the Explicitly Integrated Architecture Process

Step 1   extraction of a translation model from the program code via an implementation model;

Step 2   preparation of the translation model according to the features of the involved languages;

Step 3   translation of the translation model into a specification model.

For propagating the model changes to the code, reverse steps are executed:

Step 4   translation of the specification model into a translation model;

Step 5   preparation of the translation model according to the features of the involved languages;

Step 6   integration of the translation models with program code via an implementation model.

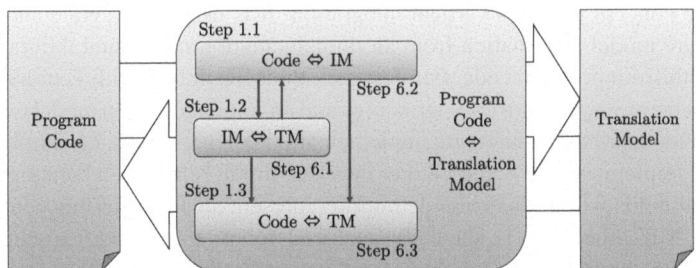

IM = Implementation Model, TM = Translation Model, ⟶ is Translated To

Fig. 3 Details of the steps 1 and 6 of the Explicitly Integrated Architecture Process

The steps 1 and 6 for model/code transformations are detailed in Fig. 3. Step 1 creates a translation model based on the program code. First, step 1.1 translates the code into an implementation model using the Model Integration Concept. Then, step 1.2 creates a translation model from the implementation model using architecture model transformations. Step 1.3 adds architecture information in the program code that cannot be expressed with the implementation model language to the translation model using the Model Integration Concept. To propagate changes in the translation model to the code, step 6.1 first translates the transformation model into an implementation model, before step 6.2 changes the code according to the changed implementation model. Step 6.3 then changes the code according to the translation model, with the architecture information that the implementation model language cannot express.

During the following steps, trace links [35] are created or used: Trace links between code and model elements are created in steps 1.1 and 1.3, and between model elements of different modeling languages in the steps 1.2 and 3. That is, in all steps from the code to the architecture specification model, trace links are created. Step 4 propagates the changes in the specification model to the translation model. The transformations require the trace links of step 3 to identify which model elements were created in step 3 and to identify changes. Step 6.1 uses the trace links of step 1.2 to propagate model changes in the translation model to the implementation model. The steps 6.2 and 6.3 use the model/code trace links of the steps 1.1 and 1.3, respectively, to identify the affected code elements. That is, during each stop during the change propagation, the corresponding traces from the model extraction are used.

2.2 Model Integration Concept

The *Model Integration Concept (MIC)*[2] describes how model information is integrated with program code. Models in the term of this approach are always based on meta models. Other models, such as mathematical functions, are not meant here. In Fig. 1 the concept provides vertical integration. It is used to integrate and extract architecture model information from an implementation model and the translation model with/from program code. For doing so, the MIC defines bidirectional formal mappings between program code structures and an implementation model expressed in a meta model of an architecture implementation language. As an example, a Java class that implements a specific marker interface might represent a component, and static final fields within this class definition represent attributes of this component. With the MIC, the code is statically analyzed for program code structures that identify implementation model elements. Changes in the model are propagated to the code, following the mapping definitions.

Figures 4 and 5 show example mappings. Figure 4 shows a meta model/code mapping for the class *Component* with the attribute *name* of the type *String*. Meta model elements are shown on the left side. The right side shows Java program code, which represents this meta model element. The meta model class is represented

---

[2]Some of the ideas behind the Model Integration Concept were first described in [14].

with the declaration of an annotation with the name `Component`. The attribute *name* is not declared in the meta model/code translation. This attribute is subject to the model/code translation in Fig. 5. The declaration of the annotation has a meta annotation `Retention`, declared `RUNTIME`, which means that the declared annotation will be part of the compiled byte code and is processable in the running system.

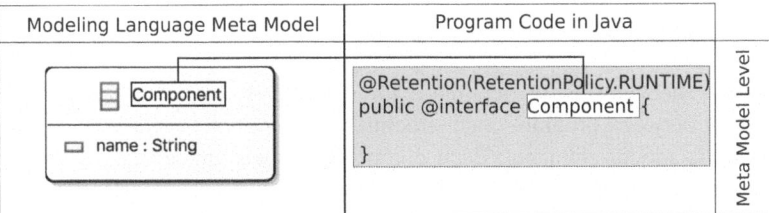

Fig. 4 An example of a meta model/code mapping

Figure 5 shows a model/code mapping for a model that instantiates the given meta model. The left side shows an instance of that meta model, a single object of the *Component* class, with the name `BarcodeScanner`. The right side shows their Java program code representation. The program code declares a type `BarcodeScanner`. The annotation `Component` is attached to the type. The type's body is a so-called *entry point*. That is, arbitrary code, such as attributes and operations, can be added here without breaking the model/code relationship.

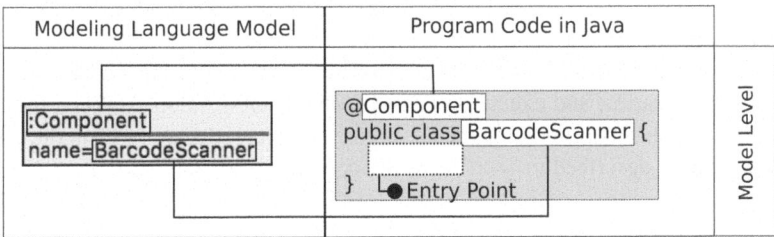

Fig. 5 An example of a model/code mapping

Such (meta) model/code mappings in the MIC are the basis for generating three types of artifacts:

1. *Bidirectional transformations* between model elements and program code build a model representation based on a given program code, so that developers can *extract* an integrated model from program code. They also have to *propagate* model changes to the code, i.e., create, delete, and change program code based on model changes. It has to be ensured that these translations are unambiguous.

2. *Meta model/code translation libraries* are program code structures, which
   represent meta model elements. In the example, this is the annotation declaration.
   This program code can be generated once. The results can be used as libraries,
   as long as the meta model does not change.
3. *Execution runtimes* can be generated for model elements. These runtimes manage
   the operational semantics of integrated models.

2.2.1 Integration Mechanisms

Integration mechanisms are templates for model/code mappings. They describe
a mapping between program code structures and symbolic meta model elements
or symbolic model elements. Each comprises a meta model/code mapping for
translating a meta model element type and a corresponding model/code mapping
for translating instances of that element. Integration mechanisms can be instantiated
by applying them to a specific meta model or model, i.e., by replacing the symbolic
elements with specific elements.

We identified 20 integration mechanisms by building upon existing Java-based
architecture implementation languages such as JEE [23] or OSGi [33]. Some are
based on the work of Moritz Balz [4]. Figures 4 and 5 show mappings for the
integration mechanism *Annotation Type* for translating objects in the model using
the Component as an example. Further mechanisms exist for objects (e.g., marker
interfaces), attributes (e.g., constant static attributes), and references (e.g., annotated
references to other objects). Konersmann's PhD thesis [12] formally describes the
current set of integration mechanisms for Java with formal definitions, examples,
and a discussion of the effects and limitations of each mechanism.

The integration mechanisms are an important part of the MIC to reduce the effort
for developing bidirectional model/code transformations and execution engines. For
integration mechanisms, reusable generic code generators for transformations, meta
model code libraries, and execution engines have been developed. When they are
instantiated with meta model elements, the respective code can be generated (see
the tool support described in Sect. 3) for the concrete mappings.

2.2.2 Operational Semantics

Two types of operational semantics exist for model elements in the context of the
MIC [13]:

1. Language semantics can be implemented in the runtime. Here each instance of a
   model element has equal semantics, e.g., when a component is instantiated, it is
   registered at a registry. These semantics apply to each component instance.
2. Model semantics can be implemented within the individual model/code structures. Here each instance of a model element has individual semantics, e.g., when

a component is instantiated, individual initialization code should be called, which can be defined by a developer.

In the latter, for executing such implementation details, translations within the MIC may declare *entry points*. Entry points may contain arbitrary code, which is not considered a part of the bidirectional model/code translation. The initialization code stated above can be implemented within operations provided by the model/code structures. An execution runtime will then execute these operations.

2.3   Intermediate Architecture Description Language

The Intermediate Architecture Description Language (IAL) mediates between architecture implementation models and architecture specification models. It has the role to increase the interoperability of the approach with different specification and implementation languages. The IAL has a small core with the common elements of architecture languages [21]. The core is extended with a variety of stereotypes to represent, e.g., different kinds of interfaces, component hierarchies, or quality attributes. Models expressed in the IAL are called *translation models*.

The core comprises the following elements: The *Architecture* is the root node that represents a software architecture comprising interconnected components. The class *ComponentType* represents a named component type. *Interfaces* can be used as an abstract definition of named interfaces for component types. Component types can provide and require interfaces. *Component Instances* represent the runtime view on components' types. The provision and requirement of interfaces is instantiated, respectively.

Profiles add further concerns to the architecture language. Such concerns include, e.g., different types of connectors, component hierarchies, types of interfaces, or quality aspects. Profiles can be categorized regarding their abstract concern, e.g., the profiles *Flat Component Hierarchy* and *Scoped Component Hierarchy* both handle the abstract concern of the component hierarchy, or *Time Resource Demand* and *Security Levels* both handle software quality concerns. Some categories are mandatory, meaning that at least one profile has to be used when an architecture is described. One kind of component-type hierarchy must be chosen. Some categories contain only optional profiles, e.g., no software quality profile is necessary to be used.

Figure 6 shows the profiles of the IAL and their interrelationships regarding their interpretation. The rectangles are categories of profiles, which share an abstract concern. The rectangles with rounded corners represent profiles. Mandatory categories (which have a solid border in Fig. 6) require at least one profile to be used. The profiles and their application are described in detail in Konersmann's PhD thesis [12]. Considering the objective of the language, in the future more profiles and categories can be added.

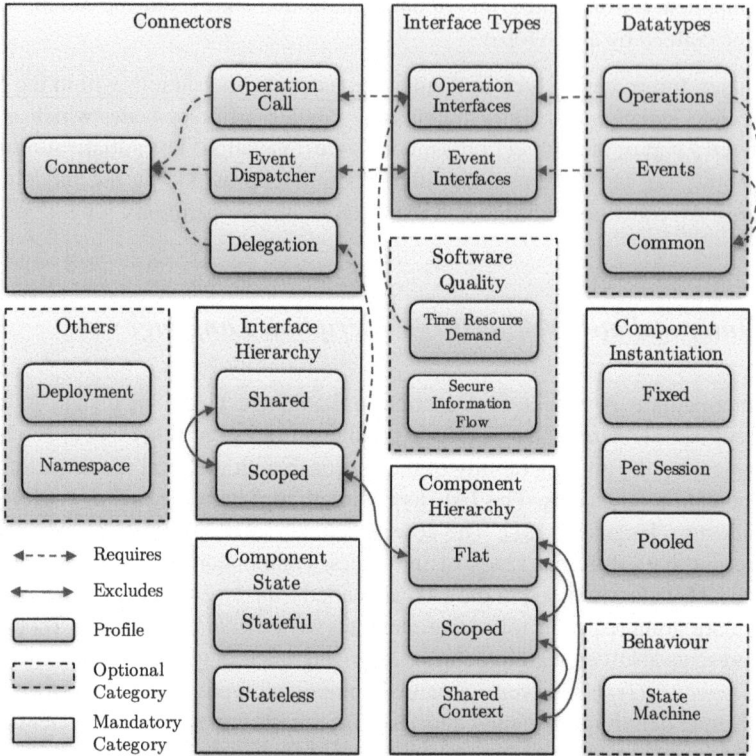

Fig. 6 An overview of profiles of the Intermediate Architecture Description Language and their interrelationships

2.4 Architecture Model Transformations

Two types of architecture model transformations are part of the EIA approach. First, transformations between architecture specification languages and the IAL as well as transformations between architecture implementation languages and the IAL are used to create a mapping between architecture specifications and implementations on a model level. Second, transformations within the IAL allow for translating between different related profiles of the IAL. In Fig. 1 the architecture model transformations provide the horizontal integration.

2.4.1 Transformations Between Architecture Languages

Transformations between architecture languages and the IAL can be defined in any model transformation technique that allows for exogenous transformations, i.e., transformations from one language to another [19].

In the implementation of the tool Codeling, we use triple graph grammars (TGGs) [26] based on attributed, typed graphs [6]. In these typed graphs, the graphs are considered models and the type graphs are meta models. A TGG describes triple rules, which declare how two graphs can be produced in alignment. They comprise a source graph, a target graph, and a correspondence graph. In our approach, one of these graphs is always a model expressed in the IAL. The triple rules are used to derive production rules and propagation rules in the context of our approach. Production rules describe how to construct a target graph from a given source graph. Propagation rules describe how to propagate changes in a target model back to the source model.

In our approach, TGGs are used:

1. to produce a translation model from an implementation model,
2. to produce an architecture specification model from the translation model,
3. to propagate changes in the specification model to the translation model, and
4. to propagate changes in the translation model to the implementation model.

We developed TGG rules for the Palladio Component Model (PCM) [5], a subset of the UML, JEE [23], and a project-specific architecture implementation language. Details on the specific rules are given in Konersmann's PhD thesis [12].

2.4.2 Transformations Within the IAL

The IAL comprises several profiles that are mutually exclusive (see Sect. 2.3). As an example, when an architecture is modeled with hierarchical component types and, at the same time, as flat component-type hierarchy, this information would be inconsistent. Nevertheless, an architecture can be expressed in an architecture implementation language that defines component-type hierarchies and should be viewed in an architecture language that can only model flat hierarchies. To respect these situations, the approach defines transformations between mutually exclusive IAL profiles, which are called *inter-profile transformations*. In the EIA process, both profiles are used in the IAL at the same time, leaving inconsistent information in the translation model. The architecture model transformations toward the target specification language only use the information they can handle, leaving trace links in the process. When changes in the specification model are translated into the translation model, the missing information is restored by exploiting the trace links. Details on the inter-profile transformations are given in Konersmann's PhD thesis [12].

3 Tool Support

We developed the following tools for the approach. Figure 7 gives an overview of the tools and their input and output. *Codeling* is the tool for executing the Explicitly

Integrated Architecture Process. It creates architecture specification model views upon program code, propagates changes in the model to the code representation, and can migrate program code from one architecture implementation language to another. Libraries in the context of Codeling support the development and execution of model/code transformations and architecture model transformations, including an automated selection and execution of inter-profile transformations.

The *code generation tool* exploits the definition of integration mechanisms for the Model Integration Concept. The tool's user maps integration mechanisms to elements of meta model elements. We developed a library of abstract transformations and execution runtimes for integration mechanisms, to decrease the effort for creating specific transformations and execution runtimes, where integration mechanisms can be applied. Based on the library of these abstract transformations and execution runtimes, the code generation tool then generates a meta model code library, model/code transformations, and execution runtime stubs.

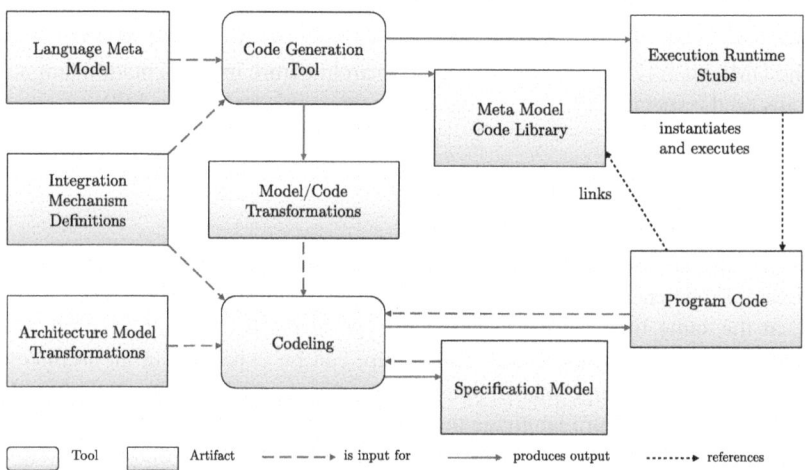

Fig. 7 An overview of the tools and the artifacts they use as input and output

3.1 Codeling

Codeling is a development and execution platform for extracting architecture models from code and for propagating changes in the models back to the code. It implements the process presented in Sect. 2.1 and provides a set of libraries to support the development of concrete transformations between program code and models.

Codeling is implemented with a modular architecture, which allows integrating further architecture implementation or specification languages, using different types of model/code or model-to-model transformation technologies.

Three types of use cases can be executed with, or are supported by Codeling:

1. For a code base, architecture specification models of different languages can be **extracted**, and **changes in these models can be propagated to the code**.
2. When a set of rules or a normative architecture exists, Codeling can extract the actual architecture from the code to **check the architectural compliance of the source code**.
3. By translating program code into the IAL and back to *another* architecture implementation language, Codeling can be a part of **software migration**. Only architecturally relevant code can be migrated. Further program code needs to be migrated by other means.

3.1.1 Model/Code Transformations

Libraries for the steps 1.1 (Code to Implementation Model), 1.3 (Code to Translation Model), 6.2 (Implementation Model to Code), and 6.3 (Translation Model to Code) of the process comprise a hierarchy of abstract classes to assist the development of concrete model/code transformations. The class hierarchy supports the transformation of Java code into Ecore [30, Chapter 5] based models and to propagate changes in the Ecore models to the Java code using the Eclipse Java Development Tools.[3]

A transformation of code into a model representation is executed in a tree structure, following containment references in the meta model: A root transformation object first translates the root code element—usually the projects at the given paths—into a model representation, the root node of the targeted model. The transformation objects store references to the code and the corresponding model element, effectively creating a trace link between the code and the model.

After the translation, the transformation object is added to a transformation object registry. This registry can be used later to retrieve model elements, which represent specific code elements or vice versa. At last, the transformation creates child transformation objects for its attributes and containment references and adds them to a pool of tasks.

Transformations for classes have transformations for their attributes and containment references as child transformations. Transformations for attributes have no child transformations. Reference transformations, including containment reference transformations, have transformations for their target objects as child references. If a containment reference is translated from a code to a model representation, the targets of the reference do not exist, because they have not been translated yet.

---

[3]Eclipse JDT—https://www.eclipse.org/jdt/.

Transformations for non-containment references first wait for the transformation of the target objects.

3.1.2 Model-to-Model Transformations

To execute model-to-model transformations between an architecture implementation or specification language and the IAL (the exogenous transformations in steps 1.2, 3, 5, and 6.1), Codeling provides helper classes to execute HenshinTGG [15] rules to create the target model or to propagate changes from a changed target model to a source model. Other technologies for defining exogenous model-transformations can also be applied, as long as change propagation is possible.

Codeling uses Henshin [6] rules for inter-profile transformations in step 2 and step 4. It derives the information about which inter-profile transformations have to be executed during the process execution. The information is based on the IAL profiles that are used in the HenshinTGG rule definitions between the IAL and the architecture implementation and specification languages.

3.1.3 Process Execution

Figure 8 shows a simple example of the Explicitly Integrated Architecture Process in action. In this example an EJB Session Bean `CashDesk` is added to an existing bean `BarcodeScanner`. The `CashDesk` is declared to be the parent of the `BarcodeScanner`.

(**1**) shows the program code for the bean `BarcodeScanner`.

(**2**) The implementation model is built by scanning the program code for mapped structures based on the Model Integration Concept. In this example a type declaration with an attached annotation `Stateless` is identified. The name of the declared type is identified as the name of the bean.

(**3**) The implementation model is translated into a translation model, an instance of the IAL.

(**4**) The translation model is translated into a specification model. The specification model in the example is represented using a UML component diagram. In an evolutionary step, a parent component named *CashDesk* is added.

The changes are propagated to the code as follows:

At (**5**) the architecture specification model is translated into the translation model. A new *ComponentType* with the name *CashDesk* is created, with a stereotype that allows to add children to a component type.

(**6**) The translation model is translated into an implementation model. In this model the hierarchy cannot be represented, because the EJB specification does not define component hierarchies.

At (**7**) the program code is adapted corresponding to the changes in the implementation model. That is, the type `CashDesk` is created.

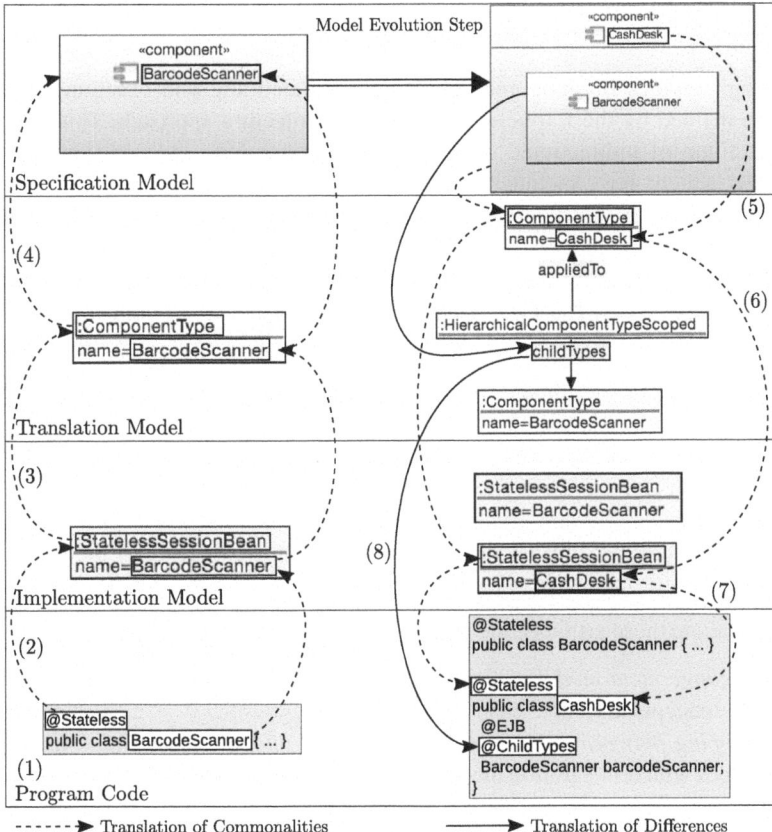

Fig. 8 An example of the Explicitly Integrated Architecture Process

(**8**) The architecture information that has no representation in the implementation model is translated into the code using the Model Integration Concept. In this example, the hierarchy is translated as a field in the Java-type declaration `BarcodeScanner` with the annotation `EJB`. This is an annotation of the EJB framework, which specifies that an instance of the bean `BarcodeScanner` has to be injected. Additionally, this field has the annotation `ChildTypes`, which marks the reference an instance of the *childTypes* reference. To remove the hierarchy, the code could be translated into a model using the process. As an alternative, the respective code element could be removed.

It should be noted that the hierarchy could also have been created in the terms of the approach by simply adapting the code accordingly, because the models can be derived automatically.

3.2   Code Generation Tool

Codeling provides libraries and components for defining and executing translations as defined by the Explicitly Integrated Architecture approach. This includes
the definition of bidirectional model/code transformations and meta model code
libraries, which, e.g., include annotations or interface definitions used by the
transformations. Developing such transformations and meta model code libraries
can be cumbersome and error-prone. The integration mechanisms can be used as
templates for generating model/code transformations and program code libraries
for meta model code. The *Code Generation Tool* generates the following artifacts
(see Fig. 7):

1. A meta model code library with code that represents architectural meta model
   elements.
2. A set of model/code transformations for extracting a model from code and
   propagating changes from the model to the code, which follow the integration
   mechanisms.
3. Execution runtime stubs for the program code that is generated by the aforementioned transformations.

   To generate these artifacts, the generator requires two items as input:

1. A *language meta model*, which describes the architecture implementation language concepts in Ecore.
2. A *mapping between meta model elements and integration mechanisms*, which
   describes which integration mechanism is to be instantiated for each meta model
   element.

   As the generated transformations follow the integration mechanisms, they reliably extract model elements from the code and propagate changes from the model
back to the code. A hierarchy of abstract classes have been prepared to add new
translations for further mechanisms. However, especially for existing component
frameworks, model/code mappings might not follow the existing integration mechanisms or require slight deviations from existing mechanisms. For these mappings,
translations have to be programmed manually, using the aforementioned hierarchy
of abstract classes. If a mapping only deviates slightly from an existing mechanism,
the generated translation can be manually adapted. In each of the use cases shown in
Sect. 4, an adaptation of generated mechanisms was necessary. For both use cases,
some translations had to be defined manually.

3.3   Execution Runtimes

Within Codeling we developed a framework for implementing execution runtimes
for models that are integrated with program code [13]. These runtimes are based

on Java's reflection mechanism to analyze the code, inject instances, and invoke operations at run-time. The framework comprises a set of abstract classes, which have to be extended for implementing specific runtime classes. For each implemented integration mechanism, an abstract runtime class exists. For implementing an execution runtime for a meta model, we map integration mechanisms to each class, reference, and attribute declared in the meta model. The code generation tool then generates an execution runtime class for each of these pairs. This creates a tree of execution runtimes, one for each meta model element. These generated execution runtime classes contain functionality to instantiate objects, set reference targets, and attribute values based on the underlying integration mechanism. The operational semantics of the modeling language can be implemented in these classes. The runtimes can effectively be seen as interpreters for the integrated models. They can also trigger operations to invoke code, which is declared in an entry point, and therefore trigger the execution of model semantics, which are expressed in program code (see Sect. 2.2.2).

4 Evaluation

For evaluation purposes, the approach has been applied in four use cases: The first use case translates the JEE program code of an e-assessment tool into a UML model with components, interfaces, operations, and their interconnection and propagates changes in the model back to the code. The second use case translates the program code of the Common Component Modeling Example (CoCoME) [10] into a subset of the Palladio Component Model (PCM) [5]. The third use case translates the CoCoME system into the UML as another architecture specification language. The fourth use case translates the CoCoME system into JEE as another architecture implementation language. In the following sections we will elaborate on the first and second use cases. All use cases are described in detail in Konersmann's PhD thesis [12].

4.1 Use Case JACK 3

In the first use case, the development of the e-assessment tool *JACK 3* is supported by generating an architectural view in the UML specification language. JACK 3 is the designated successor of the e-assessment tool JACK 2 [31], developed at the working group "Specification of Software Systems" (S3) of the institute paluno of the University of Duisburg-Essen, Germany. Its predecessor is used in the teaching and assessment of various disciplines, including programming, mathematics, and micro-economics. JACK 3 comprises two parts: a back end written in Java using the Eclipse platform as architecture implementation language, and a front end written in Java, based on the Java Enterprise Edition 7. The front end defines a user interface, data definitions, and business logic for e-assessments. The back end evaluates solutions against the defined standard solutions. It is not changed during the development of JACK 3. Therefore, this use case focuses on the front end for supporting the development of JACK 3.

This use case translates a subset of JEE technologies (EJB 3.2, CDI 1.2, and JSF 2.2) into a UML component diagram and back. JEE is a standardized set of frameworks and APIs for enterprise systems. Application servers act as execution runtimes, which analyze the code before execution, e.g., to instantiate and interconnect JEE components (beans) or to provide web-based interfaces (e.g., REST interfaces or web services). The use case also adds time resource demand information to operations in the specification model. JEE as architecture implementation language cannot express this information. This use case shows that such differences are taken into account by the approach.

For this use case, we generated and adapted model/code transformations for JEE code. The architecture implementation language JEE defines source code structures that represent architectural concepts, and platforms that execute the code. As no Ecore meta model for JEE was publicly available, we created a meta model of JEE with 11 classes, 16 references, and 22 attributes, which represent structural elements, i.e., interrelated beans and data entities in namespaces and archives, and their operations and attributes, as part of the use case.

We assigned integration mechanisms to 6 classes, 11 references, and 12 attributes. Some mechanisms had to be adapted to match the requirements of JEE-compliant code. For the other elements, we developed individual transformations based on the abstract transformations in Codeling. The project has 12307 lines of Java code (NCLOC). The resulting model has 2446 objects with 45,354 reference instances. On a computer with an Intel i5-8250U CPU and 16 GB memory on Ubuntu Linux 18.04.2 and OpenJDK version "11.0.4" 2019-07-16, the median model extraction time is about 5 s.

Furthermore, model-to-model transformations between JEE and the IAL were defined using HenshinTGG. Our TGG for JEE and the IAL comprises 35 rules. Another TGG was developed to translate between the IAL and a subset of the UML. That TGG comprises nine rules.

The extracted architecture of JACK comprises 36 UML components that are interconnected via 33 interfaces in a correctly layered architecture. It helped the developers to understand that they implemented their architecture correctly and to see how the components in the layers are interconnected. The resulting UML model is changed in the use case by adding, changing, and deleting elements. Codeling automatically changes the code according to the changes in the UML model.

Propagating a single renaming of a component, which is translated with the Type Annotation mechanism, from the UML model to the code takes about 5 s on the computer described above. The tool uses code refactoring operations to propagate this code change. For the model extraction, the main drivers for execution time are the size of the code to be analyzed and the size of the resulting model. For propagating model changes, the main drivers are the size of the model and the number of changes.

4.2 Use Case CoCoME in PCM

In the second use case, the program code of the Common Component Modeling Example (CoCoME) [10] is translated into a subset of the Palladio Component Model (PCM) [5]. CoCoME has been developed as a benchmark for comparing software architecture languages. The original CoCoME benchmark artifacts provide the context, the requirements, the design, and the implementation of a system. The system drives the business for an enterprise that runs multiple stores. Each store contains multiple cash desks in a cash desk line [10].

CoCoME does not follow a standardized implementation framework like JEE but comes with a custom style of implementing components and their interaction. This use case shows how Codeling can be applied to software that does not follow the coding conventions of industry standard platforms but follow project-specific coding conventions. In CoCoME components are implemented using Java classes with coding conventions and a set of methods to implement, alongside with a set of adjacent classes to refine the component. The code structures are not systematically implemented, so that minor changes had to be made to the code base, to define working mappings.

A meta model for the implementation structure had to be created first, before mappings could be implemented. Our meta model of CoCoME's structure contains 12 classes, 13 references, and 1 attribute. 4 classes and 4 references could be translated using integration mechanisms or variations thereof. For the other elements, we developed individual mappings based on the abstract transformations in Codeling. The project has 9425 lines of Java code (NCLOC). The resulting model has 121 objects with 1357 reference instances. On the computer described above, the median model extraction time is about 0.6 s. The first extraction takes longer (about 3 s), because the Ecore environment and the meta model need to be loaded.

4.3 Further Use Cases

The third use case translates the CoCoME code into a UML model as another architecture specification language. For this use case, we reused transformation rules between the IAL and the UML. A UML architecture description is part of the CoCoME artifacts. We extracted the UML architecture from CoCoME using our approach and compared it to the UML architecture model in the CoCoME artifacts. As the code conventions in CoCOME are not systematically implemented, the extracted architecture initially did not match with the normative architecture. Minor changes had to be made to the code base, to extract a matching architecture. This use case shows not only that architecture specifications in different languages can be extracted from the code, it also shows that, with a normative architecture specification at hand, Codeling can be used to validate the implemented architecture against an architecture specification.

The fourth use case translates the CoCoME system into JEE as another architecture implementation language. The use case shows how Codeling can be used as a part of software migrations between different architecture implementation languages. In this use case, only the steps 1 (Program Code to Translation Model), 2 (Inter-Profile Transformations), and 6 (Translation Model to Program Code) are executed. Step 1 of this use case is equal to step 1 of the CoCoME use case. In step 2 instead of targeting the UML for translation, the architecture implementation language JEE is chosen. JEE provides only a flat component hierarchy, while the CoCoME architecture implementation language uses a scoped component hierarchy. Therefore, other inter-profile transformations are executed. Steps 3 to 5 are omitted in this use case, because no architecture specification language is involved. In step 6 a TGG is applied that is close to the one that has been used in the JACK 3 use case. The JACK 3 team had special conventions how to handle Java EE code, which did not apply in the CoCoME use case. Furthermore, the same architecture implementation language meta model and model/code transformations were used as in the JACK 3 use case.

The translation results in a new project within the Eclipse IDE, with an architecture skeleton of CoCoME in JEE 7. The parent–child relationship between components in the CoCoME architecture cannot be implemented in JEE, because JEE uses flat component hierarchies. In step 6, therefore a new model/code transformation has been added, to integrate the parent–child relationship between components. A Java annotation `@Child` now indicates whether a referenced bean is the child of another bean.

4.4 Discussion

The execution of the case studies suggested that the transformations can require considerable execution times. Translating from the code to a UML representation in the JACK use case required about 225 s on the computer stated above. The backwards translation of the changed model to changes in the code required about 330 s. No information about operation parameters was included in the code-to-model translations, because the translation required multiple hours when parameters were also translated. The CoCoME case studies required 170 s for the translation to the PCM, and 140 s to the UML. The migration of CoCoME to JEE required about 210 s on the same machine. Table 1 gives an overview of the use case sizes and their performance. The number of objects and references show the IAL model size for comparison. This does not include attribute values.

The tool Codeling uses a series of code-to-model, model-to-code, and model transformations, including triple graph grammars (TGGs), to achieve its goals. TGGs can be performance intensive. Forward and backward translation rules from TGGs have a polynomial space and time complexity $O(m \times n^k)$, where m is the number of rules, n is the size of the input graph, and k is the maximum number of

Table 1 An overview of the size and performance of evaluation use cases

Use Case	No. of (Objects IAL)	No. of References (IAL)	Runtime Code to Model [s]	Runtime Model to Code [s]	Runtime Code to Code [s]
JACK 3 to UML	1644	2141	225	330	555
CoCoME to PCM	361	507	170	–	–
CoCoME to UML	361	507	140	–	–
CoCoME to JEE	361	507	–	–	210

nodes in a rule [27]. Therefore, it is expected that an increasing model size implies a higher resource demand.

A resource demand test was executed during the development of Codeling, to find the limitations of the implementation. The detailed results of the resource demand test can be found in Konersmann's PhD thesis [12]. The translation between code and specification models can be separated into the process steps for performance analysis. The main driver for time-resource demand are the TGG rules, which took about 87% of the translation time during the extraction of a synthetic model with 300 model objects. A major observation was that the TGG rules were executed on a single core. We see a high potential for reducing this time by using other model transformation techniques, especially those using parallel execution (e.g., ATL [34]).

The definition of model/code transformations for Codeling requires programming in Java or Xtend with JDT and Ecore. The code generator supports the development of model/code transformations by automatically creating transformations for meta model elements that can be translated with integration mechanisms. In our use cases some transformations have to be developed manually. Although we implemented a supporting framework (see Sect. 3), the development of transformations is not trivial. To tackle this problem, for future work we develop a language for describing mappings between model elements and source code for the Model Integration Concept, especially considering integration mechanisms. The objective is to make the development of new integration mechanisms and individual model/code transformations easier.

5   Related Work

An extensive study of literature is part of the PhD thesis. In this section we give an excerpt of the related work presented there, enriched with some more recent findings. The approach at hand is a method for extracting architecture models from code and to propagate changes in the model to the code. Pham et al. [24] describe an approach to synchronize architecture models and code. They focus on UML components and state machines as behavior models. *ReflexML* of Adersberger and Philippsen [2] is a mapping of UML component diagrams to program code artifacts, enriched with a set of consistency checks between the model and the code. Already in 1995 Murphy et al. [20] presented an approach that creates links between higher-level model elements and program code files. The general ideas behind this approach are close to the Explicitly Integrated Architecture approach. In both approaches a semantic gap between program code elements and higher-level models has been identified and should be bridged with a mapping. Codeling maps the elements on a much more fine-grained level. While these approaches allow for mapping architectural models to code elements, they are limited to a pair of languages.

The goal of *model extraction* methods is to create a model of a software design based on code or execution traces. In general, models can be extracted statically from source code and/or dynamically from execution traces [25], e.g., sequence diagrams [29], state machines [28], or software architecture from code [8]. Model extraction approaches do not aim to propagate changes to the code, but they are used for model-based analysis and communication. The MIC can be seen as a model extraction approach, extended with delta-based code generation and adaptation means.

MoDisco [7] is a tool for model-driven reverse engineering. It allows for extracting domain-specific models from code and transforming them to other code. It also comprises a Java meta model as a basis for model transformations and model-to-code transformations. MoDisco does not target architecture descriptions directly and therefore has no mechanisms for handling the differences between languages. MoDisco could be used as a basis for bidirectional model/code transformations in Codeling, but it would be necessary to add concepts for handling integration mechanisms.

Co-evolving models and code means to propagate deltas between models and code in both directions. Existing approaches use, e.g., guidelines for manual implementations [9]. Langhammer and Krogmann [17] describe an approach for the co-evolution of models of the Palladio Component Model (PCM) and Java program code, including architectural structure and abstract behavior. Langhammer [16] describes rules for correspondence relationships between the architecture model and the program code during changes on either side. Arbitrary code within methods is preserved during model-to-code change propagation. The approach is semi-automated, meaning that in cases where full automation is not possible, a developer is asked to describe how consistency can be preserved. This approach creates a specific mapping between a subset of the PCM and Java code. The MIC can conceptually be used for arbitrary meta models and programming languages, although the tools (see Sect. 3) currently support Java only.

A special case of model/code co-evolution is roundtrip engineering (RTE) [3], a method where two representations of program code are maintained together: in a textual syntax and in a—usually graphical—model syntax. RTE offers a bijective projection between the textual and the model syntax. The models used in roundtrip engineering are close to the code structures, e.g., UML class diagrams or data models. While the MIC can handle such models and their code representation, the MIC is designed to handle design models of higher abstraction levels. The MIC does not propagate code deltas to the model and is therefore not a co-evolution approach.

It is a hybrid approach of model extraction and model-code co-evolution, which extracts models and propagates model changes to code.

Balz [4] describes an approach for representing models with well-defined code structures. He defines *embedded models* as a mapping between formal models and program code patterns in a general-purpose programming language. A major contribution of Balz' work is the formal mapping between state machines and process models, and program code. It provides explicit interfaces for implanted code. The MIC is conceptually based on the essential ideas of the *embedded models* approach. Balz defines these two specific types of models for which embedded models can be used. The MIC generalizes this approach, to be usable with arbitrary meta models. With the definition of meta models as a basis, the MIC can declare integration mechanisms as templates for program code structures for reusing mappings and generate model/code transformations and execution runtime stubs.

6 Conclusions and Future Work

In this chapter we describe the Explicitly Integrated Architecture approach and its tool support. The approach extracts software architecture specifications, e.g., UML models, from source code, and propagates changes in the model to the code. It therefore creates a volatile architectural view upon the code, reducing the need to maintain two representations of the software architecture. The approach comprises four parts: (1) The Model Integration Concept is a method to extract design models from source code and propagate model changes to the code. (2) The Intermediate Architecture Description Language (IAL) is an intermediate language for translating between architecture implementations and specifications. These different views upon software architecture usually have different features for software architectures. The IAL is prepared to handle these features by using a small core and feature modules. (3) The approach translates between languages using a set of architecture model transformations, including translations between different language features, such as hierarchical and non-hierarchical architectures. (4) The Explicitly Integrated Architecture process uses the aforementioned parts to translate between source code and architecture models.

We evaluated the approach by implementing the tool Codeling accompanied by a code generator and used it in a real software project and on a benchmark software for component modeling. The evaluation has shown that the approach is usable to extract architecture specifications in different languages from a code base and to migrate an architecture implementation to another implementation language.

For future work we will develop a language to make the development of model/code transformations easier, and we evaluate other model-transformation technologies to enhance the overall performance. We are planning to evaluate the approach further on real software systems, including software with different programming languages and of different domains.

References

1. index | TIOBE - The Software Quality Company. http://web.archive.org/web/20200218103554/https://www.tiobe.com/tiobe-index/. Accessed: 2020-02-28.
2. Josef Adersberger and Michael Philippsen. ReflexML: UML-Based Architecture-to-Code Traceability and Consistency Checking. In Ivica Crnkovic, Volker Gruhn, and Matthias Book, editors, *Software Architecture - 5th European Conference, ECSA 2011, Essen, Germany, September 13–16, 2011. Proceedings*, volume 6903 of *Lecture Notes in Computer Science*, pages 344–359. Springer, 2011.
3. Uwe Aßmann. Automatic Roundtrip Engineering. *Electronic Notes in Theoretical Computer Science*, 82(5):33–41, April 2003.
4. Moritz Balz. *Embedding Model Specifications in Object-Oriented Program Code: A Bottom-up Approach for Model-based Software Development*. PhD thesis, Universität Duisburg-Essen, May 2011.
5. Steffen Becker, Heiko Koziolek, and Ralf Reussner. The Palladio component model for model-driven performance prediction. *Journal of Systems and Software*, 82:3–22, 2009.
6. Enrico Biermann, Claudia Ermel, and Gabriele Taentzer. Formal Foundation of Consistent EMF Model Transformations by Algebraic Graph Transformation. *Software & Systems Modeling*, 11(2):227–250, 2012.
7. Hugo Bruneliere, Jordi Cabot, Grégoire Dupé, and Frédéric Madiot. MoDisco: a Model Driven Reverse Engineering Framework. *Information and Software Technology*, 56(8):1012–1032, August 2014.
8. S. Ducasse and D. Pollet. Software Architecture Reconstruction: A Process-Oriented Taxonomy. *IEEE Transactions on Software Engineering*, 35(4):573–591, July 2009.
9. Thomas Haitzer, Elena Navarro, and Uwe Zdun. Reconciling software architecture and source code in support of software evolution. *Journal of Systems and Software*, 123:119–144, 2017.
10. Sebastian Herold, Holger Klus, Yannick Welsch, Constanze Deiters, Andreas Rausch, Ralf Reussner, Klaus Krogmann, Heiko Koziolek, Raffaela Mirandola, Benjamin Hummel, Michael Meisinger, and Christian Pfaller. CoCoME - The Common Component Modeling Example. chapter 3, pages 16–60. Springer-Verlag, 2008.
11. Marco Konersmann. A Process for Explicitly Integrated Software Architecture. *Softwaretechnik-Trends*, 36(2), 2016.
12. Marco Konersmann. *Explicitly Integrated Architecture - An Approach for Integrating Software Architecture Model Information with Program Code*. phdthesis, University of Duisburg-Essen, March 2018.
13. Marco Konersmann. On executable models that are integrated with program code. In *Proceedings of the 4th International Workshop on Executable Modeling co-located with ACM/IEEE 21st International Conference on Model Driven Engineering Languages and Systems (MODELS 2018), Copenhagen, Denmark, October 14, 2018.*, 2018.
14. Marco Konersmann and Michael Goedicke. A Conceptual Framework and Experimental Workbench for Architectures. In Maritta Heisel, editor, *Software Service and Application Engineering*, volume 7365 of *Lecture Notes in Computer Science*, pages 36–52. Springer Berlin Heidelberg, 2012.
15. Huu Loi Lai. Entwicklung einer Werkzeugumgebung zur Visualisierung und Analyse komplexer EMF- Modelltransformationssysteme in Henshin. Master's thesis, Tecnical University Berlin, May 2013.
16. Michael Langhammer. *Automated Coevolution of Source Code and Software Architecture Models*. Phd thesis, Karlsruhe Institute of Technology, February 2017.
17. Michael Langhammer and Klaus Krogmann. A Co-evolution Approach for Source Code and Component-based Architecture Models. *Softwaretechnik-Trends*, 35(2), 2015. ISSN 0720-8928.

18. Nenad Medvidovic and Richard N. Taylor. A Classification and Comparison Framework for Software Architecture Description Languages. *IEEE Transactions on Software Engineering*, 26(1):70–93, 2000.
19. T.a Mens and P.b Van Gorp. A Taxonomy of Model Transformation. *Electronic Notes in Theoretical Computer Science*, 152(1-2):125–142, 2006.
20. Gail C. Murphy, David Notkin, and Kevin Sullivan. Software Reflexion Models: Bridging the Gap between Source and High-Level Models. In *IEEE Transactions on Software Engineering*, pages 18–28, 1995.
21. Marco Müller. Applying Formal Component Specifications to Module Systems in Java. Master's thesis, Universität Duisburg-Essen, March 2010.
22. Marco Müller, Moritz Balz, and Michael, Goedicke. Representing Formal Component Models in OSGi. In Gregor Engels, Markus Luckey, and Wilhelm Schäfer, editors, *Software Engineering*, volume 159 of *LNI*, pages 45–56. GI, 2010.
23. Oracle America, Inc. JavaTM Platform, Enterprise Edition (Java EE) Specification, v7, June 2015. http://jcp.org/en/jsr/detail?id=342.
24. Van Cam Pham, Ansgar Radermacher, and Sébastien Gérard. A New Approach for Reflection of Code Modifications to Model in Synchronization of Architecture Design Model and Code. In Slimane Hammoudi, Luís Ferreira Pires, and Bran Selic, editors, *Proceedings of the 6th International Conference on Model-Driven Engineering and Software Development, MODELSWARD 2018, Funchal, Madeira - Portugal, January 22–24, 2018*, pages 496–503. SciTePress, 2018.
25. C. Raibulet, F. Arcelli Fontana, and M. Zanoni. Model-Driven Reverse Engineering Approaches: A Systematic Literature Review. *IEEE Access*, 5:14516–14542, 2017.
26. Andy Schürr. Specification of Graph Translators with Triple Graph Grammars. In *Graph-Theoretic Concepts in Computer Science, 20th International Workshop, WG '94, Herrsching, Germany, June 16–18, 1994, Proceedings*, pages 151–163, 1994.
27. Andy Schürr and Felix Klar. 15 Years of Triple Graph Grammars. In Hartmut Ehrig, Reiko Heckel, Grzegorz Rozenberg, and Gabriele Taentzer, editors, *Proceedings of the 4th International Conference on Graph Transformations*, volume 5214 of *Lecture Notes in Computer Science*, pages 411–425. Springer, September 2008.
28. Tamal Sen and Rajib Mall. Extracting finite state representation of Java programs. *Software and System Modeling*, 15(2):497–511, 2016.
29. Madhusudan Srinivasan, Young Lee, and Jeong Yang. Enhancing Object-Oriented Programming Comprehension Using Optimized Sequence Diagram. In *29th IEEE International Conference on Software Engineering Education and Training, CSEET 2016, Dallas, TX, USA, April 5-6, 2016*, pages 81–85. IEEE, 2016.
30. David Steinberg, Frank Budinsky, Marcelo Paternostro, and Ed Merks. *EMF: Eclipse Modeling Framework 2.0*. Addison-Wesley Professional, 2nd edition, 2009.
31. Michael Striewe. An architecture for modular grading and feedback generation for complex exercises. *Science of Computer Programming*, 129:35–47, 2016. Special issue on eLearning Software Architectures.
32. R. N. Taylor, Nenad Medvidovic, and Irvine E. Dashofy. *Software Architecture: Foundations, Theory, and Practice*. Wiley, 1 edition, January 2009.
33. The OSGi Alliance. OSGi Core. https://osgi.org/download/r6/osgi.core-7.0.0.pdf, April 2018.
34. Massimo Tisi, Salvador Martínez Perez, and Hassene Choura. Parallel execution of ATL transformation rules. In Ana Moreira, Bernhard Schätz, Jeff Gray, Antonio Vallecillo, and Peter J. Clarke, editors, *Model-Driven Engineering Languages and Systems - 16th International Conference, MODELS 2013, Miami, FL, USA, September 29 - October 4, 2013. Proceedings*, volume 8107 of *Lecture Notes in Computer Science*, pages 656–672. Springer, 2013.
35. Stefan Winkler and Jens von Pilgrim. A survey of traceability in requirements engineering and model-driven development. *Software & Systems Modeling*, 9(4):529–565, September 2010.

Actionable Program Analyses
for Improving Software Performance

Marija Selakovic

Abstract Nowadays, we have greater expectations of software than ever before. This is followed by the constant pressure to run the same program on smaller and cheaper machines. To meet this demand, the application's performance has become an essential concern in software development. Unfortunately, many applications still suffer from performance issues: coding or design errors that lead to performance degradation. However, finding performance issues is a challenging task: there is limited knowledge on how performance issues are discovered and fixed in practice, and current profilers report only where resources are spent, but not where resources are wasted. In this chapter, we investigate actionable performance analyses that help developers optimize their software by applying relatively simple code changes. We focus on optimizations that are *effective*, *exploitable*, *recurring*, and *out-of-reach for compilers*. These properties suggest that proposed optimizations lead to significant performance improvement, that they are easy to understand and apply, applicable across multiple projects, and that the compilers cannot guarantee that these optimizations always preserve the original program semantics. We implement our actionable analyses in practical tools and demonstrate their potential in improving software performance by applying relatively simple code optimizations.

1 Introduction

Regardless of the domain, software performance is one of the most important aspects of software quality: it is important to ensure an application's responsiveness, high throughput, efficient loading, scaling, and user satisfaction. Poorly performing software wastes computational resources, affects perceived quality, and increases maintenance cost. Furthermore, a web application that is perceived *slow* can result in an unsatisfied customer who may opt for a competitor's better performing product, resulting in loss of revenue.

M. Selakovic (✉)
TU Darmstadt, Darmstadt, Germany

© The Author(s) 2020
M. Felderer et al. (eds.), *Ernst Denert Award for Software Engineering 2019*,
https://doi.org/10.1007/978-3-030-58617-1_7

113

To improve software performance, three kinds of approaches have been proposed:

- *Performance profiling.* Developers conduct performance testing in the form of CPU [16] and memory profiling [20] to identify code locations that use the most resources. However, traditional profiling techniques have at least two limitations: they show where the resources are spent, but not how to optimize the program. Furthermore, they often introduce large overheads, which may affect the software's behavior and reduce the accuracy of the collected information.
- *Compiler optimizations.* Compiler optimizations [2] automatically transform a program into a semantically equivalent, yet more efficient program. However, many powerful optimization opportunities are beyond the capabilities of a typical compiler. The main reason for this is that the compiler cannot ensure that a program transformation preserves the semantics, a problem that is especially relevant for hard-to-analyze languages, such as JavaScript.
- *Manual tuning.* Finally, developers often rely on manual performance tuning [19] (e.g., manually optimizing code fragments or modifying software and hardware configurations), which can be effective but it is time consuming and often requires expert knowledge.

Limitations of existing performance analyses pose several research challenges and motivate the need for techniques that provide advice on how to improve software performance. This chapter addresses some of those limitations and proposes new approaches to help developers optimize their code with little effort.

1.1 Terminology

In this work, we use the term *actionable analysis* to denote an analysis that demonstrates the impact of implementing suggested optimization opportunities. In particular, an actionable analysis provides evidence of performance improvement (e.g., speedup in execution time or reduced memory consumption) or shows additional compiler optimizations triggered by applying a suggested optimization. Furthermore, the term *optimization* refers to a source code change that a developer applies to improve the performance of a program, and *compiler optimization* refers to an automatically applied transformation by a compiler.

1.2 Challenges and Motivation

To illustrate the potential of simple code transformations on software performance, Fig. 1 illustrates a performance issue and an associated optimization reported in *Underscore*, one of the most popular JavaScript utility libraries.

```
_.map = function(obj, iterator, context) {
  var results = [];
  if (obj == null) return results;
  _.each(obj, function(value, index, list) {
    results.push(iterator(value, index, list));
  });
  return results;
};
```

(a)

```
_.map = function(obj, iterator, context) {
  if (obj == null) return [];
  var keys = _.keys(obj);
  var length = keys.length, currentKey;
  var results = Array(length);
  for (var index = 0; index < length; index++) {
    currentKey = keys[index];
    results[index] = iterator(obj[currentKey], currentKey, obj);
  }
  return results;
};
```

(b)

Fig. 1 Performance issue from Underscore library (pull request 1708). (**a**) Performance issue. (**b**) Optimized code

Figure 1 shows the initial implementation of the *map* method, which produces a new array of values by mapping the value of each property in an object through a transformation function *iterator*. To iterate over object properties, the method uses an internal *_.each* function. However, a more efficient way is to first compute the object properties using the *keys* function and then iterate through them with a traditional for loop. The optimized version of the *map* method is shown in Fig. 1. This optimization improves performance because JavaScript engines are able to specialize the code in the for loop and execute it faster.

The optimization in Fig. 1 has four interesting properties. First, the optimization is *effective*, that is, the optimized method is on average 20% faster than the original one. Second, the optimization is *exploitable*, that is, the code transformation affects few lines of code and is easy to apply. Third, the optimization is *recurring*, that is, developers of real-world applications can apply the optimization across multiple projects. Fourth, the optimization is *out-of-reach for compilers*, that is, due to the dynamism of the JavaScript language, a compiler cannot guarantee that the code transformation is always semantics-preserving.

Detecting such optimization opportunities in a fully automatic way poses at least three challenges:

- *Understanding performance problems and how developers address them.* Despite the overall success of optimizing compilers, developers still apply manual optimizations to address performance issues in their code. The first step in building actionable performance analyses is to understand the common root causes of performance issues and code patterns that developers use to optimize their code.

- *Analysis of program behavior to detect instances of performance issues.* Based on patterns of common performance issues, the next step is to develop techniques to find code locations suffering from those issues and to suggest beneficial optimizations.
- *Exercising code transformations with enough input.* Once the actionable analysis suggests an optimization opportunity, the next step is to ensure the performance benefit of a code transformation by exercising the program with a wide range of inputs. One approach is to use manually written tests to check whether a code change brings a statistically significant improvement. However, manual tests may miss some of the important cases, which can lead to invalid conclusions. An alternative approach is to use automatically generated tests.

In this chapter, we show that *it is possible to create actionable program analyses that help developers significantly improve the performance of their software by applying effective, exploitable, recurring, and out-of-reach for compilers' optimization opportunities.* We propose novel automated approaches to support developers in optimizing their programs. The key idea is not only to pinpoint where and why time is spent but also to provide actionable advice on how to improve the application's performance.

1.3   Outline

The remaining sections of this chapter are organized as follows: Sect. 2 presents the first empirical study on performance issues and optimizations in JavaScript projects. Sections 3 and 4 present two actionable performance analyses that find reordering opportunities and method inlining optimizations. Section 5 gives an overview of the test generation approaches for higher-order functions in dynamic languages. Finally, Sect. 6 discusses conclusions and directions for future work.

2   Performance Issues and Optimizations in JavaScript

The first step in developing actionable performance analyses is to understand real-world performance issues that developers face in practice and how they address those issues. In this section, we introduce an empirical study on performance issues and optimizations in real-world JavaScript projects. We chose JavaScript because it has become one of the most popular programming languages, used not only for client-side web applications but also for server-side applications, mobile applications, and even desktop applications.

Despite the effectiveness of highly optimizing just-in-time (JIT) compilers [13, 23, 18, 9, 1], developers still manually apply optimizations to address performance issues in their code. Furthermore, future improvements of JavaScript engines are unlikely to completely erase the need for manual performance optimizations.

To find optimizations amenable for actionable performance analyses, we first need to answer the following research questions:

- RQ 1: What are the main root causes of performance issues in JavaScript?
- RQ 2: How complex are the changes that developers apply to optimize their programs?
- RQ 3: Are there recurring optimization patterns, and can they be applied automatically?

2.1 Methodology

This section summarizes the subject projects we use in the empirical study, our criteria for selecting performance issues, and our methodology for evaluating the performance impact of the optimizations applied to address these issues.

2.2 Subject Projects

We study performance issues from widely used JavaScript projects that match the following criteria:

- *Project type.* We consider both node.js projects and client-side frameworks and libraries.
- *Open source.* We consider only open source projects to enable us and others to study the source code involved in the performance issues.
- *Popularity.* For node.js projects, we select modules that are the most depended-on modules in the npm repository.[1] For client-side projects, we select from the most popular JavaScript projects on GitHub.
- *Number of reported bugs.* We focus on projects with a high number of pull requests ($\geq$ 100) to increase the chance to find performance-related issues.

Table 1 lists the studied projects, their target platforms, and the number of lines of JavaScript code. Overall, we consider 16 projects with a total of 63,951 lines of code.

---

[1]https://www.npmjs.com/browse/depended.

Table 1 Projects used for the study and the number of reproduced issues per project

Project	Description	Kind of platform	LoC	# issues
Angular.js	MVC framework	Client	7608	27
jQuery	Client-side library	Client	6348	9
Ember.js	MVC framework	Client	21, 108	11
React	Library for reactive user interfaces	Client	10, 552	5
Underscore	Utility library	Client and server	1110	12
Underscore.string	String manipulation	Client and server	901	3
Backbone	MVC framework	Client and server	1131	5
EJS	Embedded templates	Client and server	354	3
Moment	Date manipulation library	Client and server	2359	3
NodeLruCache	Caching support library	Client and server	221	1
Q	Library for asynchronous promises	Client and server	1223	1
Cheerio	jQuery implementation for server-side	Server	1268	9
Chalk	Terminal string styling library	Server	78	3
Mocha	Testing framework	Server	7843	2
Request	HTTP request client	Server	1144	2
Socket.io	Real-time application framework	Server	703	2
Total			63, 951	98

2.3 Selection of Performance Issues

We select performance issues from bug trackers as follows:

1. *Keyword-based search or explicit labels.* One of the studied projects, Angular.js, explicitly labels performance issues, so we focus on them. For all other projects, we search the title, description, and comments of issues for performance-related keywords, such as "performance," "optimization," "responsive," "fast," and "slow."
2. *Random selection or inspection of all issues.* For the project with explicit performance labels, we inspect all such issues. For all other projects, we randomly sample at least 15 issues that match the keyword-based search, or we inspect all issues if there are less than 15 matching issues.
3. *Confirmed and accepted optimizations.* We consider an optimization only if it has been accepted by the developers of the project and if it has been integrated into the code repository.
4. *Reproducibility.* We study a performance issue only if we succeed in executing a test case that exercises the code location l reported to suffer from the performance problem. We use of the following kinds of tests:

   - A test provided in the issue report that reproduces the performance problem.
   - A unit test published in the project's repository that exercises l.
   - A newly created unit test that calls an API function that triggers l.

- A newly created microbenchmark that contains the code at l, possibly prefixed by setup code required to exercise the location.

5. *Split changes into individual optimizations.* Some issues, such as complaints about the inefficiency of a particular function, are fixed by applying multiple independent optimizations. Because our study is about individual performance optimizations, we consider such issues as multiple issues, one for each independent optimization.

6. *Statistically significant improvement.* We apply the test that triggers the performance-critical code location to the versions of the project before and after applying the optimization. We measure the execution times and keep only issues where the optimization leads to a statistically significant performance improvement.

We create a new unit test or microbenchmark for the code location l only if the test is not provided or published in the project's repository. The rationale for focusing on unit tests and microbenchmarks is twofold. First, JavaScript developers extensively use microbenchmarks when deciding between different ways to implement some functionality.[2] Second, most projects we study are libraries or frameworks, and any measurement of application-level performance would be strongly influenced by our choice of the application that uses the library or framework. Instead, focusing on unit tests and microbenchmarks allows us to assess the performance impact of the changed code while minimizing other confounding factors.

In total, we select and study 98 performance issues, as listed in the last column of Table 1.

2.4 Main Findings

In this section, we discuss the main findings and provide detailed answers on the three research questions.

Root Causes of Performance Issues To address the first question, we identify eight root causes that are common among the 98 studied issues, and we assign each issue into one or more root causes. The most common root cause (52% of all issues) is that an API provides multiple functionally equivalent ways to achieve the same goal, but the API client does not use the most efficient way to achieve its goal. Figure 2b further classifies these issues by the API that is used inefficiently. For example, the most commonly misused APIs are reflection APIs, followed by string and DOM APIs.

---

[2]For example, jsperf.com is a popular microbenchmarking website.

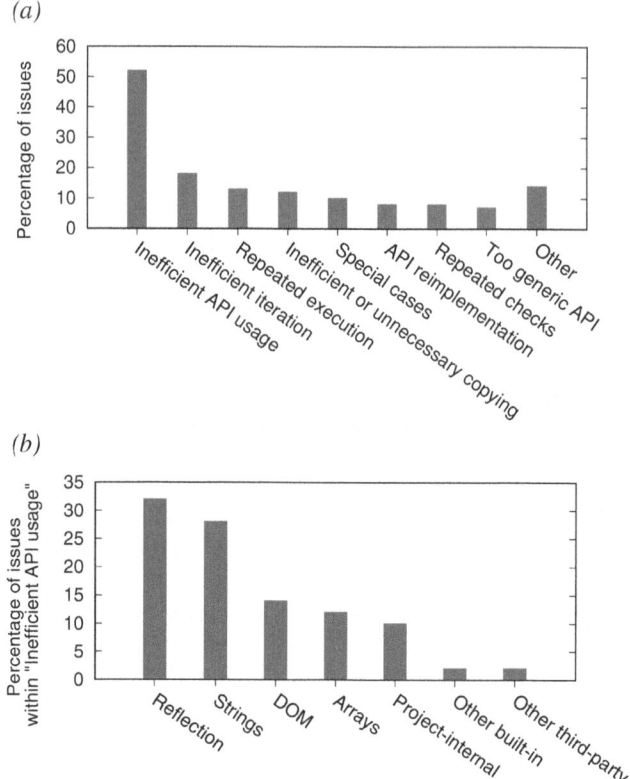

Fig. 2 Root causes of performance issues. (**a**) Most prevalent root causes. (**b**) APIs that are used inefficiently

Besides *inefficient API usage*, we identify seven other common causes of performance issues as illustrated by Fig. 2. The full description of these causes can be further found in [35], and some but not all of them have been addressed by existing approaches for automatically finding performance problems [15, 38, 39]. However, our results suggest that there is a need for additional techniques to help developers find and fix instances of other common performance issues.

Complexity of Changes To better understand to what degree optimizations influence the complexity of the source code of the optimized program, we measure the number of statements in the program and the cyclomatic complexity [24] of the program before and after each change. These metrics approximate the understandability and maintainability of the code.

Figure 3a, b summarizes our results. The graphs show what percentage of optimizations affect the number of statements and the cyclomatic complexity in a particular range. We find that a large portion of all optimizations do not affect the

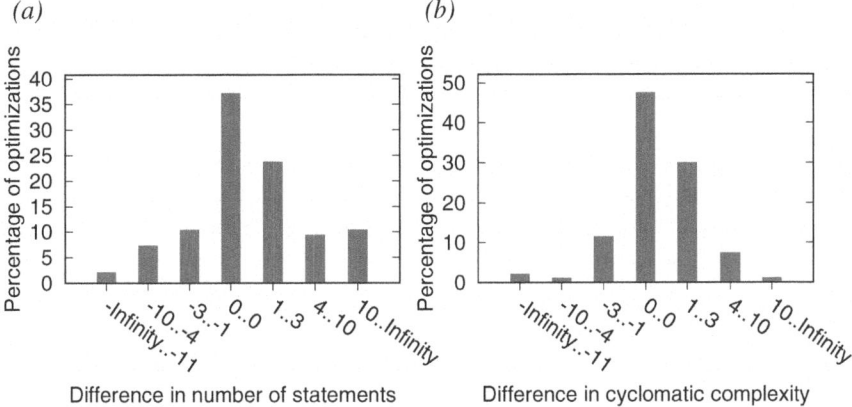

Fig. 3 Effect of applying an optimization on the cyclomatic complexity. (**a**) Effect on the number of statements. (**b**) Effect on cyclomatic complexity

number of statements and the cyclomatic complexity at all: 37.11% do not modify the number of statements, and 47.42% do not modify the cyclomatic complexity. It is also interesting to note that a non-negligible percentage of optimizations decreases the number of statements (19.59%) and the cyclomatic complexity (14.43%).

These results challenge the common belief that optimizations come at the cost of reduced code understandability and maintainability [22, 11]. We conclude from these results that many optimizations are possible without increasing the complexity of the optimized program.

Recurring Optimization Patterns To identify performance optimizations that may apply in more than a single situation, we inspect all studied issues. First, we identify optimizations that occur repeatedly within the study. Furthermore, since some issues may not expose multiple instances of a pattern that would occur repeatedly in a larger set, we also identify patterns that may occur repeatedly. To find whether there are occurrences of the optimization patterns beyond the 98 studied optimizations, we develop a simple, AST-based, static analysis for each pattern and apply it to programs used in the study.

We find that the analyses cannot guarantee that the optimization patterns can be applied in a fully automated way without changing the program's semantics due to the following features of JavaScript language:

- *Dynamic types*: the types of identifiers and variables can be dynamically changed.
- *Dynamic changes of object prototypes*: properties of object prototype can be dynamically overridden.
- *Dynamic changes of native methods*: native or third-party functions can be dynamically overridden.

For example, in Fig. 1, the `obj` identifier must always have `Object` type, the `hasOwnProperty` property of `Object.prototype` must not be overridden, and both `hasOwnProperty()` and `keys()` must be built-in JavaScript functions.

To check whether a match is a valid optimization opportunity, the analyses also rewrite the program by applying the respective optimization pattern. We then manually inspect the rewritten program and prune changes that would modify the program's semantics. In total, we find 139 new instances of recurring optimization patterns, not only across single project but also across multiple projects. These results motivate the research and the development of techniques that help developers apply an already performed optimizations at other code locations, possibly along the lines of existing work [26, 27, 3].

2.5 Practical Impact

The results of the empirical study can help improve JavaScript's performance by providing at least three kinds of insights. First, application developers benefit by learning from mistakes made by others. Second, developers of performance-related program analyses and profiling tools benefit from better understanding what kinds of problems exist in practice and how developers address them. Third, developers of JavaScript engines benefit from learning about recurring bottlenecks that an engine may want to address and by better understanding how performance issues evolve over time.

3 Performance Profiling for Optimizing Orders of Evaluation

The previous section discusses the most common performance problems and optimizations in JavaScript projects. It shows that many optimizations are instances of relatively simple, recurring patterns that significantly improve the performance of a program without increasing code complexity. However, automatically detecting and applying such optimization opportunities are challenging due to the dynamic features of the JavaScript language.

Reordering Opportunities In this section, we focus on a recurring and easy to exploit optimization opportunity called *reordering opportunity*. A reordering opportunity optimizes the orders of conditions that are part of a decision made by the program. As an example, Fig. 4 shows an instance of reported reordering optimization in a popular JavaScript project. The code in Fig. 4 checks three conditions: whether a regular expression matches a given string, whether the value stored in `match[3]` is defined, and whether the value of `arg` is greater than or equal to zero. This code can be optimized by swapping the first two expressions

```
arg = (/[def]/.test(match[8]) && match[3] && arg >= 0 ? '+'+ arg : arg);
```

(a)

```
arg = (match[3] && /[def]/.test(match[8]) && arg >= 0 ? '+'+ arg : arg);
```

(b)

Fig. 4 Performance issues from Underscore.string (pull request 471). (**a**) Optimization opportunity. (**b**) Optimized code

(Fig. 4) because checking the first condition is more expensive than checking the second condition. After this change, when match[3] evaluates to false, the overall execution time of evaluating the logical expression is reduced by the time needed to perform the regular expression matching.

Once detected, such opportunities are easy to exploit by reordering the conditions so that the cost of overall evaluation has the least possible cost. At the same time, such a change often does not sacrifice readability or maintainability of the code. Beyond the examples in Fig. 4, we found various other reordering optimizations in real-world code,[3] including several reported by us to the respective developers.[4]

3.1 An Analysis for Detecting Reordering Opportunities

Challenges Even though the basic idea of reordering conditions is simple, detecting reordering opportunities in real-world programs turns out to be non-trivial. We identify three challenges.

- *Measuring the cost and likelihood of conditions.* To identify reorderings of conditions that reduce the overall cost of evaluations, we must assess the cost of evaluating individual expressions and the likelihood that an expression evaluates to true. The most realistic way to assess computational cost is to measure the actual execution time. However, short execution times cannot be measured accurately. To compute the optimal evaluation order, we require an effective measure of computational cost, which should be a good predictor of actual execution time while being measurable with reasonable overhead.
- *Analyze all conditions.* To reason about all possible reorderings, we must gather cost and likelihood information for all conditions. However, dynamically analyzing all conditions may not be necessary in a normal execution. For example, consider that the first condition in Fig. 4 evaluates to false. In this case,

---

[3]For example, see jQuery pull request #1560.
[4]For example, see Underscore pull request #2496 and Moment pull request #3112.

Fig. 5 Overview of
DecisionProf

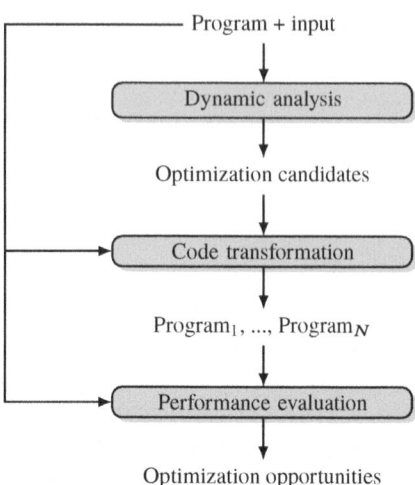

the overall value of the expression is determined as `false`, without executing the
other two conditions.

- *Side effect-free evaluation of condition.* Evaluating conditions may have side
  effects, such as modifying a global variable or an object property. Therefore,
  naively evaluating all conditions, even though they would not be evaluated in
  the normal program execution, may change the program's semantics. To address
  this issue, we need a technique for evaluating individual expressions without
  permanently affecting the state of the program.

DecisionProf: An Overview To address the aforementioned challenges, we propose *DecisionProf*, a profiling approach that automatically finds reordering opportunities at runtime and proposes them to the developer. Figure 8 gives an overview of
the approach. The input to *DecisionProf* is an executable program and the output is
the list of reordering opportunities. The first step of the profiler is a dynamic analysis
that identifies optimization candidates. In the second step, for each candidate, the
approach applies the optimization via source-to-source transformation. Finally, for
the modified version of the program, *DecisionProf* checks whether an optimization
reduces the execution time of a program. If and only if the changes lead to
statistically significant performance improvement, the approach suggests them as
reordering opportunities to the developer (Fig. 5).

3.2 Dynamic Analysis

The main component of *DecisionProf* is the runtime analysis that collects two
pieces of information about every dynamic occurrence of a condition: the computational *cost* of evaluating the condition and the *value*, i.e., whether the Boolean

expression evaluates to `true` or `false`. *DecisionProf* gathers these runtime data in two steps. At first, it statically preprocesses the source code of the analyzed program. More details on a preprocessing step can be found in [34]. After collecting runtime data, the approach associates with each condition a cost-value history:

Definition 1 (Cost-Value Histories) The cost-value history h of a condition is a sequence of tuples (c, v), where v denotes the value of the condition and c represents the cost of evaluating the condition. The cost-value histories of all conditions are summarized in a history map $\mathcal{H}$ that assigns a history to each condition.

To gather cost-value histories, the analysis reacts to particular runtime events:

- When the analysis observes a beginning of a new conditional statement, it pushes the upcoming evaluation onto a stack *evaluations* of currently evaluated statement.
- When the analysis observes new condition, it pushes the condition that is going to be evaluated onto a stack *conditions* of currently evaluated conditions. Furthermore, the analysis initializes the cost c of the upcoming evaluation to one.
- When reaching a branching point, the analysis increments the cost counter c of each condition in *conditions*. We use the number of executed branching points as a proxy measure for wall clock execution time, avoiding the challenges of reliably measuring short-running code.
- When the analysis observes the end of conditional evaluation, it pops the corresponding condition from *conditions*. Furthermore, the analysis appends (c, v) to h, where h is the cost-value history of the condition as stored in the history map $\mathcal{H}$ of *top(evaluations)*, c is the cost of the current condition evaluation, and v is the Boolean outcome.
- When reaching the end of conditional statements, the analysis pops the corresponding statement from *evaluations*.

The reason for using stacks to represent the currently evaluated conditions is that they may be nested. For example, consider a logical expression `a() || b ()`, where the implementation of `a` contains another complex logical expression.

Our approach refines the described analysis in two ways. First, the analysis monitors runtime exceptions that might occur during the evaluation of the Boolean expression. If an exception is thrown, the analysis catches the error, restores the program state, and excludes the expression from further analysis. Such exceptions typically occur because the evaluation of one condition depends on the evaluation of another condition. Second, the analysis considers switch statements with case blocks that are not terminated with a `break` or `return` statement. For such case blocks, the analysis merges conditions corresponding to the cases that are evaluated together into a single condition.

Based on cost-value histories obtained through dynamic analysis, *DecisionProf* computes an optimal order of conditions for each executed conditional statement in the program. The computed order is optimal in the sense that it minimizes the overall cost of the analyzed executions.

Table 2 Cost-value histories from executions of Fig. 4

Check	Execution		
	First	Second	Third
/[def]/.test(match[8])	(3, true)	(3, true)	(3, false)
match[3]	(1, true)	(1, false)	(1, false)
arg	(1, true)	(1, true)	(1, true)

To illustrate the algorithm for finding the optimal order of conditions, consider Table 2 that shows a cost-value history gathered from three executions of the logical expression in Fig. 4. For example, when the logical expression was executed for the first time, the check /[def]/.test(match[8]) was evaluated to true and obtaining this value imposed a runtime cost of 3. Based on these histories, the algorithm computes the optimal cost of the first, innermost logical expression, /[def]/.test(match[8]) && match[3]. The costs in the three executions with the original order are 4, 4, and 3. In contrast, the costs when swapping the conditions are 4, 1, and 1. That is, swapping the subexpressions reduces the overall cost. Therefore, the optimal order for the first subexpression is match[3] && /[def]/.test(match[8]). Next, the algorithm moves up in the expression tree and optimizes the order of match[3] && /[def]/.test(match[8]) and arg. Comparing their costs shows that swapping these subexpressions is not beneficial, so the algorithm computes the history of the subexpression, and finally it returns match[3] && /[def]/.test(match[8]) && arg as the optimized expression.

3.3 Experimental Evaluation

We evaluate the effectiveness and efficiency of *DecisionProf* by applying it to 43 JavaScript projects: 9 widely used libraries and 34 benchmark programs from the JetStream suite, which is commonly used to assess JavaScript performance. To execute the libraries, we use their test suites, which consist mostly of unit-level tests. We assume for the evaluation that these inputs are representative for the profiled code base. The general problem of finding representative inputs to profile a given program [17, 5, 10] is further discussed in Sect. 5.

Table 3 illustrates the libraries and benchmarks used in the evaluation. In total, *DecisionProf* detects 52 reordering opportunities. The column "Optimizations" in Table 3 shows how many optimizations the approach suggests in each project and function-level performance improvements after applying these optimizations. To the best of our knowledge, none of the optimizations detected by *DecisionProf* have been previously reported. Furthermore, after manually inspecting all suggested optimizations, we find that all of them are semantics-preserving, i.e., the approach has no false positives in our evaluation. Further details on detected opportunities, examples, and their performance impact can be found in [34].

Table 3 Projects used for the evaluation of *DecisionProf*

Project	Tests	LoC	Optimizations	Perf. improvements (%)
Libraries				
Underscore	161	1110	2	3.7–14
Underscore.string	56	905	1	3–5.8
Moment	441	2689	1	3–14.6
Minimist	50	201	1	4.2–6.5
Semver	28	863	5	3.5–10.6
Marked	51	928	1	3–4.4
EJS	72	549	2	5.6–6.7
Cheerio	567	1396	9	6.2–40
Validator	90	1657	3	3–10.9
Total	1516	10, 928	23	
Benchmarks				
float-m		3972	3	2.5
crypto-aes		295	3	5.2
deltablue		483	2	6.5
gbemu		9481	18	5.8
Total		14, 231	26	

Reported Optimizations To validate our hypothesis that developers are interested in optimizations related to the order of checks, we reported a small subset of all detected reordering opportunities. Three out of seven reported optimizations got confirmed and fixed within a very short time, confirming our hypothesis.

4   Cross-Language Optimizations in Big Data Systems

Sections 2 and 3 illustrate how relatively small code changes can significantly improve the execution time of JavaScript applications. While this is true for JavaScript-based web applications, frameworks, and libraries, the question is whether similar findings hold for complex, distributed applications that run simultaneously on multiple machines.

In this section, we demonstrate the potential of the *method inlining* code optimization in a large-scale data processing system. Method inlining is a simple program transformation that replaces a function call with the body of the function. We search for method inlining opportunities in programs written in SCOPE [7], a language for big data processing queries that combines SQL-like declarative language with C# expressions.

To demonstrate the effectiveness of method inlining, Fig. 6 illustrates two semantically equivalent SCOPE programs that interleave relational logic with C# expressions. Figure 6a shows the situation where the user implements the predicate

Fig. 6 Examples of SCOPE programs. (**a**) Predicate invisible to optimizer. (**b**) Predicate visible to optimizer

```
data = SELECT *
    FROM inputStream
    WHERE M(A, B);

#CS
bool M(string x, string y) {
    return !String.IsNullOrEmpty(x) && y == "Key1";
}
#ENDCS
```

(a)

```
data = SELECT *
    FROM inputStream
    WHERE !String.IsNullOrEmpty(A) AND B == "Key1";
```

(b)

in the WHERE clause as a separate C# method. Unfortunately, the presence of non-relational code blocks the powerful relational optimizations in the SCOPE compiler. As a result, the predicate is executed in a C# virtual machine. On the other hand, Fig. 6 shows a slight variation where the user *inlines* the method body in the WHERE clause. Now, the predicate is amenable to two potential optimizations:

1. The optimizer may choose to *promote* one (or both) of the conjuncts to an earlier part of the script, especially if either A or B is the column used for partitioning the data. This can dramatically reduce the amount of data needed to be transferred across the network.
2. The SCOPE compiler has a set of methods that it considers to be *intrinsic*. An intrinsic is a .NET method for which the SCOPE runtime has a semantically equivalent native function, i.e., implemented in C++. For instance, the method String.isNullOrEmpty checks whether its argument is either null or else the empty string. The corresponding native method is able to execute on the native data encoding, which does not involve creating any .NET objects or instantiating the .NET virtual machine.

The resulting optimizations improve the throughput of the SCOPE program by 90% percent.

4.1 Performance Issues in SCOPE Language

SCOPE [7] is a big data query language, and it combines a familiar SQL-like declarative language with the extensibility and programmability provided by C# types and the C# expression language. In addition to C# expressions, SCOPE allows user-defined functions (*UDFs*) and user-defined operators (*UDOs*). Each operator, however, must execute either entirely in C# or in C++: mixed code is not provided for. Thus, when possible, the C++ operator is preferred because the data layout in stored data uses C++ data structures. But when a script contains a C# expression that cannot be converted to a C++ function, such as in Fig. 6a, the .NET runtime must be started and each row in the input table must be converted to a C# representation.

Data conversions to and from .NET runtime poses a significant cost in the overall system. To alleviate some of these inefficiencies, the SCOPE runtime contains C++ functions that are semantically equivalent to a subset of the .NET framework methods that are frequently used; these are called *intrinsics*. Wherever possible, the SCOPE compiler emits calls to the (C++) intrinsics instead of C# functions. However, the optimization opportunity presented in Fig. 6 is outside the scope of SCOPE compiler: user-written functions are compiled as a black box: no analysis or optimization is performed at this level.

4.2 Static Analysis to Find Method Inlining Opportunities

SCOPE jobs run on a distributed computing platform, called Cosmos, designed for storing and analyzing massive data sets. Cosmos runs on five clusters consisting of thousands of commodity servers [7]. Cosmos is highly scalable and performant: it stores exabytes of data across hundreds of thousands of physical machines. Cosmos runs millions of big data jobs every week and almost half a million jobs every day.

Finding optimization opportunities in such a large number of diverse jobs is a challenging problem. We can hope to find interesting conclusions only if our analysis infrastructure is scalable. To achieve this, we analyze the following artifacts that are produced after the execution of each SCOPE program:

- *Job Algebra* The job algebra is a graph representation of the job execution plan. Each vertex in a graph contains operators that run either inside native (C++) or .NET runtime.
- *Runtime Statistics* The runtime statistics provide information on the CPU time for every job vertex and every operator inside the vertex.
- *Generated Code* The SCOPE compiler generates both C# and C++ codes for every job. An artifact containing the C++ code has for every vertex a code region containing a C++ implementation of the vertex and another code region that provides class names for every operator that runs as C#. An artifact containing the C# code includes implementations of non-native operators and user-written classes and functions defined inside the script.

The first step of the analysis is to extract the names of each job vertex, which serves as a unique identifier for the vertex. Then, for each vertex, the analysis parses the generated C++ to find the class containing the vertex implementation. If in the class the list of C# operators is empty, we conclude that the entire vertex runs as C++ code. Otherwise, the analysis outputs class names that contain C# operators. Then, it parses C# code to find definition and implementation for every class name. For a non-native operator, there are two possible sources of C# code: generated code, which we whitelist and skip in our analysis and the user-written code. After analyzing user code, the final sources of C# code are *.NET framework calls, user-written functions,* and *user-written operators.*

To find method inlining opportunities, we are particularly interested in the second category. Among user-written functions, we find inlineable ones as per the following definition:

Definition 2 (Inlineable Method) Method m is *inlineable* if it has the following properties:

- It contains only calls to *intrinsics* methods
- It does not contain loops and try-catch blocks
- It does not contain any assignment statements.
- It does not contain any references to the fields of an object.
- For all calls inside the method, arguments are passed by value (i.e., no *out* parameters or call-by-reference parameters).

By optimizing inlineable methods, the SCOPE compiler is now able to run the operator contains the method completely in native runtime. In the next section, we further discuss the empirical results of performance improvements due to method inlining opportunities. The complete description of our analysis infrastructure can be found in [33].

4.3 Experimental Evaluation

To understand the potential of method inlining opportunities, we analyze over 3,000,000 SCOPE jobs over a period of six days that run on five data centers at Microsoft. To quantify the amount of CPU time that can be optimized by applying method inlinings, we consider job vertices that have as the only source of managed code an *inlineable* method. By optimizing such a method, we expect an entire vertex to run as native code, which should significantly improve the vertex execution time. Figure 7 shows the proportion of CPU time of optimizable vertices relative to data center time and total time spent in .NET runtime. We observe that with the current list of intrinsics, we can optimize a relatively small proportion of both, data center time and non-native time. For example, in cosmos9 that runs the most expensive jobs, we can optimize at most 0.01% of data center time. The situation is slightly better in cosmos14 or cosmos15, where we can optimize up to 0.15% of data center time. However, taking into account the scale of big data processing at Microsoft, this percentage amounts to almost 40,000 h of optimizable time.

The crucial observation is that the results illustrate only the time in data centers that can be affected by inlining method calls. To measure the actual performance improvement, it is necessary to rerun every optimized job.

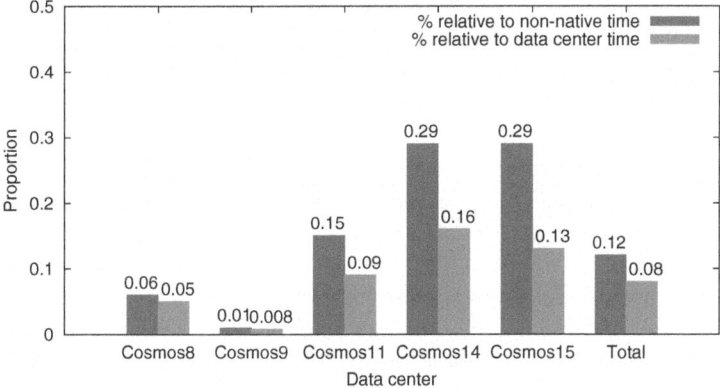

Fig. 7 Execution time affected by method inlining

Table 4 Summary of case studies. The reported changes are percentage of improvements in CPU time and throughput

Job name	C++ translation	Job cost	CPU time		Throughput
			Vertex change	Job change	
A	Yes	Medium	59.63%	23.00%	30%
B	Yes	Medium	No change	No change	No change
C	Yes	Low	41.98%	25.00%	38%
D	No	–	–	–	–
E	Yes	High	7.22%	4.79%	5%
F	Yes	Low	No change	No change	115%

4.3.1 Case Studies

In order to quantify the effects of optimizing the SCOPE scripts through method inlining, we performed several case studies. We reported jobs that have *optimizable vertices*, meaning that the job owner can optimize the script by inlining a method that calls only intrinsics.

Because the input data for each job are not available, we had to contact the job owners and ask them to rerun the job with a manually inlined version of their script. We were able to have 6 jobs rerun by their owners, categorized by their total CPU time: short, medium, and long.

In total, we looked at 6 rerun jobs, summarized in Table 4. For one job (D), the optimization did not trigger C++ translation of an inlined operator because the operator called to a non-intrinsic method that we mistakenly thought was an intrinsic. After detecting this problem, we fix the set of intrinsics and use the new set to obtain data presented in this section.

For jobs A and B, we were able to perform the historical study over a period of 18 days. Both jobs are medium-expensive jobs, run daily, and contain exactly one optimizable vertex due to user-written functions. In both cases, inlining the function resulted in the entire vertex being executed in C++. The values are normalized by the average of the unoptimized execution times; the optimized version of the job A saves approximately 60% of the execution time. In similar fashion, we find that the normalized vertex CPU time in Job B does not show any consistent improvement. Closer analysis of the vertex shows that the operator which had been in C# accounted for a very tiny percentage of the execution time for the vertex. This is in line with our results for Job A, where the operator had essentially been 100% of the execution time of the vertex.

We also optimized Job F, a very low-cost job. It only runs a few times a month, so we were able to obtain timing information for only a few executions. The vertex containing the optimized operator accounted for over 99% of the overall CPU time for the entire job. We found the CPU time to be highly variable; perhaps, this is because the job runs so quickly, so it is more sensitive to the batch environment in which it runs. However, we found the throughput measurements to be consistent: the optimized version provided twice the throughput for the entire job (again, compared to the average of the unoptimized version).

Finally, for jobs C and E, we were not able to perform the same kind of historical study: instead, we have just one execution of the optimized scripts. For this execution, we found improvements in both vertex and job CPU times.

By presenting six case studies of big data processing tasks, we show that method inlinig is a promising optimization strategy for triggering more generation of native code in SCOPE programs, which yields significant performance improvements.

5 Test Generation of Higher-Order Functions in Dynamic Languages

In Sect. 3, we present *DecisionProf*, a dynamic analysis for optimizing inefficient orders of evaluations. To find reordering opportunities, *DecisionProf* relies on inputs provided by test suites. Similarly, other dynamic analyses are applied with manually written tests or by manually exploring the program. However, such inputs are often not sufficient to cover all possible program paths or to trigger behavior that is of interest to the dynamic analysis.

To address the problem of insufficient test inputs, a possible solution is to use test generation in combination with dynamic analysis. Automatically generated tests can either extend manual tests or serve as the sole driver to execute applications during dynamic analysis. Existing test generation uses a wide range of techniques, including feedback-directed random testing [29, 30], symbolic execution [21, 6], concolic execution [14, 37], bounded exhaustive testing [4], evolutionary test generation [12], UI-level test generation [25, 28, 34], and concurrency testing [31, 32].

For dynamic analysis to be precise, test generation must provide high-quality test cases. This means that generated tests should exercise as many execution paths as possible and achieve good code coverage. However, despite their effectiveness in identifying programming errors, current test generation approaches have limited capabilities in generating structurally complex inputs [40]. In particular, they do not consider higher-order functions that are common in functional-style programming, e.g., the popular map or reduce APIs, and in dynamic languages, e.g., methods that compose behavior via synchronous or asynchronous callbacks.

Testing a higher-order function requires the construction of tests that invoke the function with values that include callback functions. To be effective, these callback functions must interact with the tested code, e.g., by manipulating the program's state. Existing test generators do not address the problem of higher-order functions at all or pass very simple callback functions that do not implement any behavior or return random values [8].

The problem of generating higher-order functions is further compounded for dynamically typed languages, such as JavaScript, Python, and Ruby. For these languages, in addition to the problem of creating an effective callback function, a test generator faces the challenge of determining where to pass a function as an argument. Addressing this challenge is non-trivial in the absence of static type signatures.

In this section, we give a brief overview of *LambdaTester*, a novel framework for testing higher-order functions in dynamic languages. The complete details of the framework and proposed solution can be found in [36].

5.1 Overview of the Framework

In the *LambdaTester* framework, test generation proceeds in two phases. The *discovery phase* is concerned with discovering, for a given method under test m, at which argument position(s) the method expects a callback function. To this end, the framework generates tests that invoke m with callback functions that report whether or not they are invoked. Then, the *test generation phase* creates tests that consist of a sequence of calls that invoke m with randomly selected values, including function values at argument positions where the previous phase discovered that functions are expected. The test generation phase uses a form of feedback-directed, random testing [29] to incrementally extend and execute tests. We augment feedback-directed, random testing with four techniques to create callback arguments. Both phases take as input setup code that creates a set of initial values, which are used as receivers and arguments in subsequently generated calls.

The basic ingredient of generated tests is method calls:

Definition 3 (Method Call) A method call c is a tuple $(m, var_{rec}, var_{arg1} \cdots var_{argn}, var_{return})$, where m is a method name, var_{rec} is the name of the variable used as the receiver object of the call, $var_{arg1}, \ldots, var_{argk}$ are the names of variables used as arguments, and var_{return} is the name of the variable to which the call's return value is assigned.

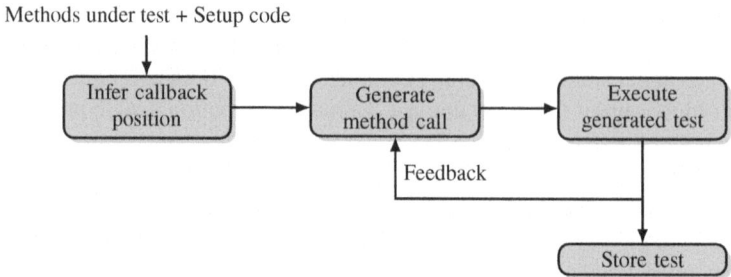

Methods under test + Setup code

Fig. 8 Overview of *LambdaTester*

Finally, the overall goal of the approach is to generate tests:

Definition 4 (Test) A test *test* is a sequence $(setup, c_i, \ldots, c_n)$, where *setup* is the setup code and $c_i, \ldots, c_n$ are generated method calls.

Figure 8 illustrates the process of test generation. For each method under test, the approach attempts to infer the positions of callback arguments. Afterward, the approach repeatedly generates new method calls and executes the growing test. During each test execution, the approach collects feedback that guides the generation of the next method call. Finally, the approach stores the generated tests, which can then be used as an input to the dynamic analysis or for bug finding [36].

5.2   Callback Generation Approaches

The key idea of *LambdaTester* is a feedback-directed test generation with a novel generation of callback inputs. Our framework currently supports four techniques for generating callback functions, which we present below.

Empty Callbacks The most simple approach for creating callbacks is to simply create an empty function that does not perform any computation and does not explicitly return any value. Figure 9 gives an example of an empty callback.

Callbacks by QuickCheck QuickCheck [8] is a state-of-the-art test generator originally designed for functional languages. To test higher-order functions, QuickCheck is capable of generating functions that return random values, but the functions that it generates do not perform additional computations and do not modify the program state. Figure 9 gives an example of a callback generated by QuickCheck.

Existing Callbacks Given the huge amount of existing code written in popular languages, another way to obtain callback functions is to extract them from already written code. To find existing callbacks for a method *m*, the approach statically analyzes method calls in a corpus of code and extracts function expressions passed

```
function callback() {
};
```

(a)

```
function callback() {
  return 17;
};
```

(b)

```
function callback() {
  return Math.floor(10.8) +
         Math.floor(20.4) +
         Math.min(3, 5);
};
```

(c)

```
function callback(a,b) {
  receiver.foo = "abc"
  b = null;
  return {x: 23};
};
```

(d)

Fig. 9 Examples of generated callbacks. (**a**) Empty callback ("Cb-Empty"). (**b**) Callback generated by QuickCheck ("Cb-QuickCheck"). (**c**) Callback mined from existing code ("Cb-Mined"). (**d**) Callback generated based on dynamically analyzing the method under test ("Cb-Writes")

to methods with a name equal to m. For example, to test the map function of arrays in JavaScript, we search for callback functions given to map. The rationale for extracting callbacks specifically for a each method m is that callbacks for a specific API method may follow common usage patterns, which may be valuable for testing these API methods.

Callbacks Generation Based on Dynamic Analysis The final and most sophisticated technique to create callbacks uses a dynamic analysis of the method under test to guide the construction of a suitable callback function. The technique is based on the observation that callbacks are more likely to be effective for testing when they interact with the tested code. To illustrate this observation, consider the following method under test:

```
function testMe(callbackFn, bar) {
  // code before calling the callback

  // calling the callback
  var ret = callbackFn();

  // code after calling the callback
  if (this.foo) { ... }
  if (bar) { ... }
  if (ret) { ... }
}
```

To effectively test this method, the callback function should interact with the code executed after invoking the callback. Specifically, the callback function should modify the values stored in this.foo, ret, and bar. The challenge is how to determine the memory locations that the callback should modify.

We address this challenge through a dynamic analysis of memory locations that the method under test reads after invoking the callback. We apply the analysis when executing tests and feed the resulting set of memory locations back to the test generator to direct the generation of future callbacks. The basic idea behind the dynamic analysis is to collect all memory locations that (i) are read after the first invocation of the callback function and (ii) are reachable from the callback body. The reachable memory locations include memory reachable from the receiver object and the arguments of the call to the method under test, the return value of the callback, and any globally reachable state.

For the above example, the set of dynamically detected memory locations is { receiver.foo, arg2, ret }.

Based on detected memory locations, *LambdaTester* generates a callback body that interacts with the function under test. To this end, the approach first infers how many arguments a callback function receives. Then, *LambdaTester* generates callback functions that write to the locations read by the method under test and that are reachable from the callback body. The approach randomly selects a subset of the received arguments and of the detected memory locations and assigns a random value to each element in the subset.

Figure 9 shows a callback function generated for the above example, based on the assumption that the callback function receives two arguments. As illustrated by the example, the feedback from the dynamic analysis allows *LambdaTester* to generate callbacks that interact with the tested code by writing to memory locations that are relevant for the method under test.

As further discussed in [36], all callback generation techniques are more effective in finding programming errors than state-of-the-art test generation approaches that do not consider the generation of function inputs. Moreover, among proposed techniques, generating callbacks that modify program state in non-obvious ways is more effective in triggering non-trivial executions than other callback generation techniques.

6 Conclusions

In this chapter, we present actionable program analyses to improve software performance. More concretely, we focus on an empirical study of the most common performance issues in JavaScript programs (Sect. 2), analyses to find reordering opportunities (Sect. 3) and method inlining opportunities (Sect. 4), and a novel test generation technique for higher-order functions in dynamic languages (Sect. 5). These approaches aim to reduce manual effort by suggesting only beneficial optimization opportunities that are easy to understand and applicable across multiple projects.

6.1 Summary of Contributions

We show that it is possible to automatically suggest effective, exploitable, recurring, and out-of-reach for compilers' optimization opportunities. In particular,

- By empirically studying performance issues and optimizations in real-world software, we show that most issues are addressed by optimizations that modify only a few lines of code, without significantly affecting the complexity of the source code. Furthermore, we observe that many optimizations are instances of patterns applicable across projects. These results motivate the development of performance-related techniques that address relevant performance problems.
- Applying these optimizations in a fully automatic way is a challenging task: they are subject to preconditions that are hard to check or can be checked only at runtime. We propose two program analyses that prove to be powerful in finding optimization opportunities in complex programs. Even though our approaches do not guarantee that code transformations are semantics-preserving, the experimental results illustrate that suggested optimizations do not change program behavior.
- Reliably finding optimization opportunities and measuring their performance benefits require a program to be exercised with sufficient inputs. One possible solution to this problem is to use automated test generation techniques. We complement existing testing approaches by addressing the problem of test generation for higher-order functions. Finally, we show that generating effective tests for higher-order functions triggers behaviors that are usually not triggered by state-of-the-art testing approaches.

6.2 Future Research Directions

Assessing Performance Impact Across Engines Reliably assessing the performance benefits of applied optimizations is a challenging task, especially if a program runs in multiple environments. Optimization strategies greatly differ across different engines and also across different versions of the same engine. To make sure that optimizations lead to positive performance improvements in all engines, future work should focus on techniques that monitor the performance effects of code changes across multiple execution environments.

Automatically Identifying Optimization Patterns Existing approaches that address performance bottlenecks either look for general performance properties, such as hot functions, or for specific patterns of performance issues. As already shown in Sects. 3 and 4, finding and applying specific optimization opportunities can lead to significant performance improvements. However, this requires manually identifying optimization patterns and hard-coding them into the respective analysis. Manually studying instances of inefficient code and finding recurring patterns are challenging tasks that often require significant human effort. Even though we studied a significant number of performance problems and drew interesting conclusions in Chap. 2, the next interesting research question is *How to automatically find optimization patterns that have significant performance benefits and are applicable across multiple projects?*

Analyses to Find Other Optimization Opportunities We propose approaches that address two different types of optimizations: reordering opportunities and method inlining. However, in Sect. 2, we discuss many optimization patterns that have the same properties as those we address. Therefore, it is an important research direction to propose novel approaches that address other kinds of performance issues and provide actionable advices to developers.

References

1. W. Ahn, J. Choi, T. Shull, M. J. Garzarán, and J. Torrellas. Improving JavaScript performance by deconstructing the type system. In *Conference on Programming Language Design and Implementation (PLDI)*, pages 496–507, 2014.
2. A. V. Aho, R. Sethi, and J. D. Ullman. *Compilers. Principles, Techniques and Tools*. Addison Wesley, 1986.
3. M. Boshernitsan, S. L. Graham, and M. A. Hearst. Aligning development tools with the way programmers think about code changes. In *CHI*, pages 567–576, 2007.
4. C. Boyapati, S. Khurshid, and D. Marinov. Korat: automated testing based on Java predicates. In *International Symposium on Software Testing and Analysis (ISSTA)*, pages 123–133, 2002.
5. J. Burnim, S. Juvekar, and K. Sen. WISE: Automated test generation for worst-case complexity. In *ICSE*, pages 463–473. IEEE, 2009.
6. C. Cadar, D. Dunbar, and D. R. Engler. KLEE: Unassisted and automatic generation of high-coverage tests for complex systems programs. In *Symposium on Operating Systems Design and Implementation (OSDI)*, pages 209–224. USENIX, 2008.
7. R. Chaiken, B. Jenkins, P. Larson, B. Ramsey, D. Shakib, S. Weaver, and J. Zhou. Scope: Easy and efficient parallel processing of massive data sets. *Proc. VLDB Endow.*, 1(2):1265–1276, Aug. 2008.
8. K. Claessen and J. Hughes. Quickcheck: A lightweight tool for random testing of Haskell programs. *SIGPLAN Not.*, 46(4):53–64, May 2011.
9. I. Costa, P. Alves, H. N. Santos, and F. M. Q. Pereira. Just-in-time value specialization. In *CGO*, pages 1–11, 2013.
10. M. Dhok and M. K. Ramanathan. Directed test generation to detect loop inefficiencies. In *FSE*, 2016.
11. R. R. Dumke, C. Rautenstrauch, A. Schmietendorf, and A. Scholz, editors. *Performance Engineering, State of the Art and Current Trends*, London, UK, UK, 2001. Springer-Verlag.
12. G. Fraser and A. Arcuri. Evosuite: automatic test suite generation for object-oriented software. In *SIGSOFT/FSE'11 19th ACM SIGSOFT Symposium on the Foundations of Software Engineering (FSE-19) and ESEC'11: 13th European Software Engineering Conference (ESEC-13), Szeged, Hungary, September 5–9, 2011*, pages 416–419, 2011.
13. A. Gal, B. Eich, M. Shaver, D. Anderson, D. Mandelin, M. R. Haghighat, B. Kaplan, G. Hoare, B. Zbarsky, J. Orendorff, J. Ruderman, E. W. Smith, R. Reitmaier, M. Bebenita, M. Chang, and M. Franz. Trace-based just-in-time type specialization for dynamic languages. In *PLDI*, pages 465–478, 2009.

14. P. Godefroid, N. Klarlund, and K. Sen. DART: directed automated random testing. In *Conference on Programming Language Design and Implementation (PLDI)*, pages 213–223. ACM, 2005.
15. L. Gong, M. Pradel, and K. Sen. JITProf: Pinpointing JIT-unfriendly JavaScript code. In *European Software Engineering Conference and Symposium on the Foundations of Software Engineering (ESEC/FSE)*, pages 357–368, 2015.
16. S. L. Graham, P. B. Kessler, and M. K. Mckusick. Gprof: A call graph execution profiler. In *SIGPLAN Symposium on Compiler Construction*, pages 120–126. ACM, 1982.
17. M. Grechanik, C. Fu, and Q. Xie. Automatically finding performance problems with feedback-directed learning software testing. In *International Conference on Software Engineering (ICSE)*, pages 156–166, 2012.
18. B. Hackett and S. Guo. Fast and precise hybrid type inference for JavaScript. In *Conference on Programming Language Design and Implementation (PLDI)*, pages 239–250. ACM, 2012.
19. A. Hartono, B. Norris, and P. Sadayappan. Annotation-based empirical performance tuning using orio. *2009 IEEE International Symposium on Parallel & Distributed Processing*, pages 1–11, 2009.
20. S. H. Jensen, M. Sridharan, K. Sen, and S. Chandra. Meminsight: platform-independent memory debugging for javascript. In *Proceedings of the 2015 10th Joint Meeting on Foundations of Software Engineering, ESEC/FSE 2015, Bergamo, Italy, August 30 - September 4, 2015*, pages 345–356, 2015.
21. J. C. King. Symbolic execution and program testing. *Communications of the ACM*, 19(7):385–394, 1976.
22. D. E. Knuth. Computer programming as an art. *Commun. ACM*, 17(12):667–673, Dec. 1974.
23. F. Logozzo and H. Venter. RATA: Rapid atomic type analysis by abstract interpretation—application to JavaScript optimization. In *CC*, pages 66–83, 2010.
24. T. J. McCabe. A complexity measure. *IEEE Transactions on Software Engineering*, 2(4):308–320, Dec. 1976.
25. A. M. Memon. An event-flow model of GUI-based applications for testing. *Softw. Test., Verif. Reliab.*, pages 137–157, 2007.
26. N. Meng, M. Kim, and K. S. McKinley. Systematic editing: generating program transformations from an example. In *PLDI*, pages 329–342, 2011.
27. N. Meng, M. Kim, and K. S. McKinley. Lase: locating and applying systematic edits by learning from examples. In *ICSE*, pages 502–511, 2013.
28. A. Mesbah and A. van Deursen. Invariant-based automatic testing of Ajax user interfaces. In *ICSE*, pages 210–220, 2009.
29. C. Pacheco and M. D. Ernst. Randoop: Feedback-directed random testing for java. In *Companion to the 22Nd ACM SIGPLAN Conference on Object-oriented Programming Systems and Applications Companion*, OOPSLA '07, pages 815–816, New York, NY, USA, 2007. ACM.
30. C. Pacheco, S. K. Lahiri, and T. Ball. Finding errors in .NET with feedback-directed random testing. In *International Symposium on Software Testing and Analysis (ISSTA)*, pages 87–96. ACM, 2008.
31. M. Pradel and T. R. Gross. Fully automatic and precise detection of thread safety violations. In *Conference on Programming Language Design and Implementation (PLDI)*, pages 521–530, 2012.
32. M. Samak and M. K. Ramanathan. Multithreaded test synthesis for deadlock detection. In *Conference on Object-Oriented Programming Systems, Languages and Applications (OOPSLA)*, pages 473–489, 2014.
33. M. Selakovic, M. Barnett, M. Musuvathi, and T. Mytkowicz. Cross-language optimizations in big data systems: A case study of scope. In *Proceedings of the 40th International Conference on Software Engineering: Software Engineering in Practice*, ICSE-SEIP '18, pages 45–54, New York, NY, USA, 2018. ACM.

34. M. Selakovic, T. Glaser, and M. Pradel. An actionable performance profiler for optimizing the order of evaluations. In *International Symposium on Software Testing and Analysis (ISSTA)*, pages 170–180, 2017.
35. M. Selakovic and M. Pradel. Performance issues and optimizations in JavaScript: An empirical study. In *International Conference on Software Engineering (ICSE)*, pages 61–72, 2016.
36. M. Selakovic, M. Pradel, R. Karim, and F. Tip. Test generation for higher-order functions in dynamic languages. *Proceedings of the ACM on Programming Languages*, 2:1–27, 10 2018.
37. K. Sen, D. Marinov, and G. Agha. Cute: A concolic unit testing engine for c. In *Proceedings of the 10th European Software Engineering Conference Held Jointly with 13th ACM SIGSOFT International Symposium on Foundations of Software Engineering*, ESEC/FSE-13, pages 263–272, New York, NY, USA, 2005. ACM.
38. L. D. Toffola, M. Pradel, and T. R. Gross. Performance problems you can fix: A dynamic analysis of memoization opportunities. In *Conference on Object-Oriented Programming, Systems, Languages, and Applications (OOPSLA)*, pages 607–622, 2015.
39. G. H. Xu, N. Mitchell, M. Arnold, A. Rountev, E. Schonberg, and G. Sevitsky. Finding low-utility data structures. In *Conference on Programming Language Design and Implementation (PLDI)*, pages 174–186, 2010.
40. H. Zhong, L. Zhang, and S. Khurshid. Combinatorial generation of structurally complex test inputs for commercial software applications. In *Proceedings of the 2016 24th ACM SIGSOFT International Symposium on Foundations of Software Engineering*, FSE 2016, pages 981–986, New York, NY, USA, 2016. ACM.

.

The manufacturer's authorised representative in the EU is Springer
Nature Customer Service Centre GmbH, Europaplatz 3, 69115 Heidelberg,
Germany. If you have any concerns regarding our products, please
contact ProductSafety@springernature.com

Printed and bound by CPI Group (UK) Ltd, Croydon, CR0 4YY
07/05/2026
02104586-0002